Physical Characteristics of the Chesapeake Bay Retriever

(excerpted from the American Kennel Club)

Body: Of medium length, neither cobby nor roached, but rather approaching hollowness from underneath as the flanks should be well tucked up.

Back: Short, well coupled and powerful.

Topline: Should show the hindquarters to be as high as or a trifle higher than the shoulders.

Tail: Of medium length; medium heavy at the base. The tail should be straight or slightly curved.

Hindquarters: Should be especially powerful to supply the driving power for swimming. Legs should be medium length and straight, showing good bone and muscle. Stifles should be well angulated.

Weight: Males should weigh 65 to 80 pounds; females should weigh 55 to 70 pounds.

Height: Males should measure 23 to 26 inches; females should measure 21 to 24 inches.

Color: As nearly that of its working surroundings as possible. Any color of brown, sedge or deadgrass is acceptable, self-colored Chesapeakes being preferred.

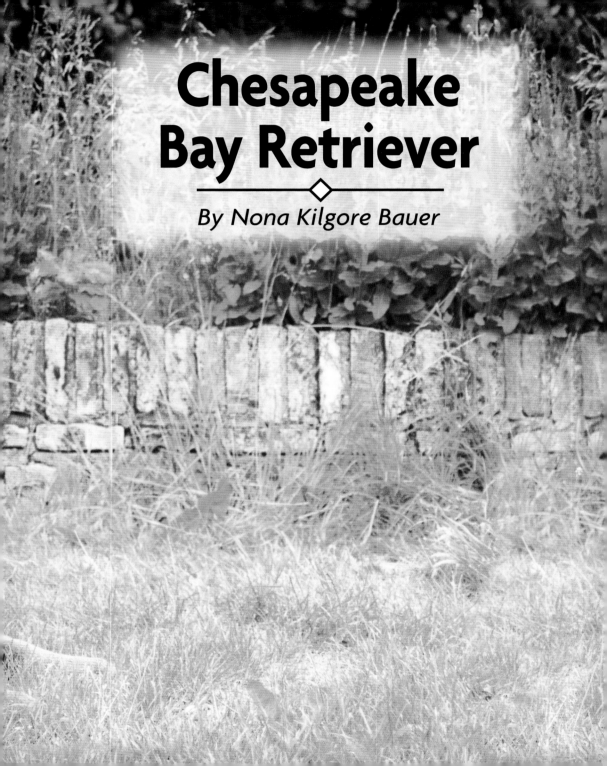

Chesapeake Bay Retriever

By Nona Kilgore Bauer

9   History of the Chesapeake Bay Retriever

Meet the talented and rugged retriever from the shores of Maryland. Learn about the origins and development of the "Chesapeake Bay Ducking Dog," and follow the breed's amazing feats in the field, on the water and in competition. Not just a "wavy Labrador," the Chessie stands apart from the other retriever breeds in both looks and personality.

23   Characteristics of the Chesapeake Bay Retriever

Steady, intelligent, skilled and loyal, the Chesapeake is without equal as a hunting partner and, with the right owners, as a companion. Do you have what it takes to own, train and provide for the active, sometimes stubborn, but immensely lovable Chessie? Personality, owner suitability and breed-specific health concerns are among the topics discussed.

30   Breed Standard for the Chesapeake Bay Retriever

Learn the requirements of a well-bred Chesapeake Bay Retriever by studying the description of the breed as set forth in the American Kennel Club's breed standard. Both show dogs and pets must possess key characteristics as outlined in the standard.

37   Your Puppy Chesapeake Bay Retriever

Be advised about choosing a reputable breeder and selecting a healthy, typical puppy. Understand the responsibilities of ownership, including home preparation, acclimatization, the vet and prevention of common puppy problems.

63   Everyday Care of Your Chesapeake Bay Retriever

Enter into a sensible discussion of dietary and feeding considerations, exercise, grooming, traveling and identification of your dog. This chapter discusses Chesapeake Bay Retriever care for all stages of development.

78   Training Your Chesapeake Bay Retriever

By Charlotte Schwartz
Be informed about the importance of training your Chesapeake Bay Retriever from the basics of house-training and understanding the development of a young dog to executing obedience commands (sit, stay, down, etc.).

Contents

KENNEL CLUB BOOKS® **CHESAPEAKE BAY RETRIEVER**
ISBN: 1-59378-338-8

Copyright © 2004, 2007 • Kennel Club Books® • A Division of BowTie, Inc.
40 Main Street, Freehold, NJ 07728 USA
Cover Design Patented: US 6,435,559 B2 • Printed in South Korea

10 9 8 7 6 5 4 3 2

Photography by Carol Ann Johnson, with additional photographs by:

Norvia Behling, T.J. Calhoun, Carolina Biological Supply, Doskocil, Isabelle Français, James Hayden-Yoav, James R. Hayden, RBP, Bill Jonas, Dwight R. Kuhn, Dr. Dennis Kunkel, Mikki Pet Products, Phototake, Jean Claude Revy, Dr. Andrew Spielman and Alice van Kempen.

Illustrations by Patricia Peters.

The publisher wishes to thank owners Patsy Barber, Carol F. Cassity, Johanna L. Dewaldt, Kathleen Luthy, Janet Morris, Ruth Ann Leigh-Phillips & J. R. Phillips and Joanne Silver.

HISTORY OF THE
CHESAPEAKE BAY RETRIEVER

Few Sporting breeds can boast a history as colorful as the Chesapeake Bay Retriever, beginning with a shipwreck in stormy seas off the coast of Maryland and two rescued Newfoundland pups who became legends in the Chesapeake Bay area for their extraordinary feats of courage while retrieving wounded waterfowl. Today the 21st-century descendants of those original "Chesapeake Bay Ducking Dogs" still retrieve with the same prowess and tenacity as their fabled ancestors.

The breed's ancestry dates back to 1739, with reports of powerful and courageous dogs that retrieved great numbers of shot game from the rough and icy waters of the Chesapeake Bay. Documents from that time tell us about fearless retrieving exploits performed by dogs called water spaniels, a type of dog considered by some historians to be of Spanish origin. In that single respect, all retriever breeds, including the Chesapeake, may share a common ancestry, being descendants of those Spanish dogs. Over the next three

A waterfowl retriever that derives from the Chesapeake Bay area of Maryland, the Chesapeake Bay Retriever performs today with the same spectacular ability as his forebears.

100/—

Newfoundland

Uganda

The Newfoundland swims at the heart of the Chesapeake Bay Retriever's origins, according to the popular folklore of the region. The Newfoundland is celebrated and revered around the world, as this postage stamp from Uganda, saluting life-saving water dogs, indicates.

centuries, the water spaniels were crossed with various setters, hounds and Newfoundlands to produce the retriever breeds we recognize today: the Golden, Labrador, Flat-Coated, Curly-Coated, Nova Scotia Duck Tolling and, of course, Chesapeake Bay.

Leaping ahead to the autumn of 1807, two St. John's Newfound-land puppies were said to be aboard an English ship that was carrying a load of codfish from Newfoundland back to Poole, England. The pups were unrelated and had been selected by their breeder from prime breeding stock. Historians speculate that the pups were probably on their way to the estate of the English nobleman, Lord Malmesbury, who at that time was attempting to develop a specific strain of retriever-type hunting dog.

During its voyage, the vessel encountered a heavy gale off the coast of Maryland and, unable to weather the fierce storm, began to

sink. Good fortune prevailed, however, when an American ship named the *Canton* came upon the scene. The *Canton*, owned by Mr. Hugh Thompson, was steaming toward its homeport in Baltimore, Maryland, with Mr. Thompson's nephew, Mr. George Law, one of the passengers aboard. Mr. Law assisted with the rescue of the English ship's crew and cargo, including the two pups. He subsequently purchased the pups from the English captain and named the black bitch Canton, after his uncle's ship, and called the male, who was red in color, Sailor.

Arriving at his Baltimore destination, Mr. Law presented Canton to Dr. James Stewart of Sparrow's Point and gave Sailor to Mr. John Mercer of West River. Although they lived on opposite shores of the Chesapeake Bay, both men were ardent hunters who trained and used the dogs for duck retrieving. Accordingly, Sailor and Canton soon became known on both coasts as exceptional water retrievers. Both dogs had uncommonly thick, coarse haircoats that rendered them impervious to the icy waters of the Chesapeake Bay. Although rather small in stature, the dogs possessed courage, strength, tenacity and endurance that were unsurpassed in duck shooting.

Mr. Mercer also told of Sailor's eyes, which he called

"...very peculiar, so light as to have an almost unnatural appearance, and...nearly 20 years later...many of his descendants were marked with this same peculiarity." Sailor was later purchased by Maryland's Governor Lloyd, who used him extensively for hunting as well as for breeding at his estate on the eastern shore of Maryland. Sailor's offspring became well known for their superior performance as ducking dogs, and for many years were referred to as the Sailor breed.

Canton remained with Dr. Stewart until her death, performing extraordinary feats of strength and courage while at Sparrow's Point. She was relentless in her pursuit of wounded birds, battling with crippled swans and swimming after wounded ducks for miles through ice and fog. Author T. S. Skinner wrote of Canton, "When she was most fatigued, she climbed on a cake of floating ice, and after resting herself on it, she renewed her pursuit of the ducks."

Since both dogs were well known for their retrieving ability and their skill and stamina working in the ice-choked waters, they were much sought after by local duck and market hunters. Their progeny inherited their superb qualities and, by the mid-1800s, the breed was clearly distinguishable. Of those off-

spring, Skinner wrote, "In their descendants, even to the present remote generation, the fine qualities of the original pair are conspicuously preserved, in spite of occasional strains of inferior blood."

Although Canton and Sailor were never bred to each other, they are still considered to be the original ancestors of the Chesapeake Bay Retriever. While numerous theories exist about which crossbreedings were instrumental in defining and enhancing the present distinctive qualities of the breed, two requirements were paramount in the breeding of Bay-area hunting dogs: a fanatical retriever and a dull, dark coat to blend with the dog's surroundings. Thus, many hunting and

ONE BREED UNDIVIDED
Of all the retriever breeds, only the Chesapeake has not split into two different types, with one type bred specifically for the hunter and the other for the show ring.

The Curly-Coated Retriever, along with other breeds, has been cited in the makeup of the Chesapeake Bay Retriever. The coat of the Curly certainly may have contributed to the Chessie's impenetrable waterproof jacket.

water breeds would logically have been used as breeding stock.

Written references indicate crosses with Irish Water Spaniels, Curly-Coated and Flat-Coated Retrievers, some setter breeds and yellow and tan coonhounds. While several types of dog evolved, the superior qualities of the early Chesapeake prevailed. All along both shores of the Chesapeake Bay, a very definite ducking dog emerged, one of superior courage, strength and endurance, capable of mile-long swims, often retrieving 200 ducks a day in snow, ice and heavy seas. Under such extreme conditions, a weak dog simply did not survive.

To fully appreciate the exceptional performance of the

Chesapeake Bay Retriever at his work, you must understand the geography of Maryland's Bay area. The northeastern coastal region in which the state is located is home to harsh winters, with huge numbers of migratory birds flying over the icy waters of the Bay. Indeed, shooting was commonly profuse, frequently with over a dozen downed ducks to retrieve at one time, forcing the dogs to go back again and again to find crippled and wounded birds.

These hardy dogs were in demand by the professional market hunters, whose profession and demeanor necessitated the utmost from a working dog. Gunning in the rough and icy seas of the Bay area was a tough game, and early tales abound about Chesapeakes who gave their lives in frigid waters while they relentlessly pursued, killed or crippled ducks that were drifting away with the tide. It is evident that the Chesapeake that developed in this area was no accident, but rather the result of careful breeding by the hunters and families who valued the breed's special qualities.

Given their popularity, many great lines of Chesapeake Bay dogs developed during the early 1800s, and the breed became known by several names: the Bay Duck Dog, the Otter Dog, the Winchester Ducking Dog and the Chesapeake Bay Ducking Dog, with the latter name prevailing into the late 19th century.

In the 1870s, a class of Chesapeake Bay Ducking Dogs was shown at the Poultry and Fanciers Association in Baltimore, with dogs entered from both the eastern and western shores of the Bay. Although unrelated, the dogs' likeness to one another was so striking that a group of sportsmen pondered the issue of whether the Chesapeake Bay Ducking Dog could be considered a specific

Evidence points to the Irish Water Spaniel, prized for its athleticism and swimming acumen, as being among the breeds crossed to the Chessie.

breed. Since it had originated in a crossbreeding, they questioned whether a breed bearing similar coat and color could be reproduced every time. They ultimately divided the breed into three classes: the otter dog, which carried a wavy brown coat of tawny sedge coloring; the curly dog and the straight-haired dog, which were both red-brown in color. Thus was born the first recognized, albeit rather loose, standard for the breed.

During the mid- to late 1800s, the Chesapeake Bay Ducking Dog was the favorite of the Carroll Island Gun Club, which was located along the Gunpowder River near Baltimore. Club members hunted over Chesapeakes exclusively and bred their dogs selectively. They often played host to wealthy sportsmen and politicians who had a penchant for serious hunting and hardy hunting dogs, thus promoting the breed's special qualities beyond their local shores.

For many years, the club held the official pedigree of the Chesapeake Bay Dog, and by 1887 a definite strain had evolved, a dog that carried a dark brown color that faded into reddish sedge. The deadgrass coloration, as one of the Chesapeake's colors is called today, was unknown at that time. Regrettably, at the turn of the century, a fire at the club destroyed all of their breeding records.

The National American Kennel Club (NAKC) was founded in 1876. The first Chesapeake Bay Dog was registered with that organization in 1878, a male named Sunday, bred by O.D. Foulks and owned by G.E. Keirstead of LaPorte, Indiana. When the NAKC was reorganized into American Kennel Club (AKC) six years later in 1884, it accepted registrations of Chesapeake Bay Dogs, making the Chesapeake the first of the retriever breeds to be recognized by the AKC. For the next 40-plus years, all other retriever breeds except the Chesapeake were lumped together in one class until the AKC finally separated them into the breeds we know today.

The Chesapeake breeding program followed by the Carroll Island club and other gun clubs on the coast appears to have been the greatest influence in the development of a breed of uniform type with distinct characteristics. The intended breed blended the three original types— otter dog, curly dog and straight-

---

GUNPOWDER RIVER DOGS

The early Chesapeake used in the breeding program on the western shore of the Chesapeake Bay was sometimes called the Gunpowder River Dog.

The Chesapeake Bay Retriever became the American Kennel Club's first registered retriever breed.

haired dog—proposed by that first group of sportsmen. Club members, led by General Ferdinand C. Latrobe, joined with other Chesapeake fanciers to form the Baltimore Chesapeake Bay Dog Club. In 1890, their organization created their own standard for the Chesapeake Bay Dog, and by the early 1900s word of the breed's prowess as a hunter had spread beyond the shores of Maryland, reaching north and west into Canada and beyond.

The American Chesapeake Club was formed in 1918 by Mr. Earl Henry of Albert Lea, Minnesota. Mr. Henry had bred Chesapeakes since 1888, and by 1901 he had developed his own strain of the deadgrass color.

Concerned about rising breed popularity and the future of the breed, Mr. Henry joined with Mr. W.H. Orr of Mason City, Iowa, a Mr. F.E. Richmond and several other fanciers to form a national breed club to protect and improve breed uniformity and emphasize working ability. The group drew up a new standard, which was offered to over 50 breeders in the United States and Canada for approval. The American Chesapeake Club thus became the beacon for the Chesapeake breed, and their standard was accepted and approved by the American Kennel Club. AKC registrations from 1934 show a total of 283 retrievers registered during that year and, of that total, 103 were

Chesapeakes, proof that in those days, the Chessie was the hunter's favored retriever.

The American Chesapeake Club hosted the breed's first field trial, for Chessies only, at the Chesapeake national specialty in 1932, 14 years after the club's inception. During those early years, the Chesapeake competed most ably in all-breed field trials, running against Labradors, Goldens, Curly-Coated Retrievers and Irish Water Spaniels. The specialty field trial continued annually until World War II began in 1941. Then, as happened with all other dog breeds, the war interfered with breeding and breed activities throughout the 1940s.

During the pre-war years, breed popularity spread eventually to the West-Coast states and, in 1920, Mr. Orr furnished breeding stock to breeder William Wallace Dougall of San Francisco, who had taken a fancy to the breed. Other prominent

Chesapeake breeders of that time included Iowa residents Harry Carney and D.W. Dawson, and South Dakotans J.L. Schmidt and the famous retriever trainer Charles Morgan.

On the East Coast, Chesacroft Kennels of Lutherville, Maryland had linebred Chesapeakes for 50 years. In 1932, Anthony Bliss of Long Island purchased the Chesacroft operation. Two years later, Bliss became president of the American Chesapeake Club, and his enthusiasm and leadership inspired many Chesapeake breeders and fanciers to establish their own kennels. Mr. Bliss owned 8 of the 40 Chesapeakes who attained championship status between 1930 and 1940.

Despite the hardships of World War II, American Kennel Club registrations continued to increase slowly every year. In 1938, there were only 178 individual Chesapeake registrations; by 1945, there were 427; by 1950, the number had climbed to 543.

During the next several decades, the Chesapeake flourished in all areas of canine competition. Through the 1980s, 7 breed members earned both FC (Field Champion) and AFC (Amateur Field Champion) titles, with 11 FC and 11 AFC titles also awarded. By that time, a total of 11 Chessies had also become Dual Champions, earning their FC and

AFC as well as their Champion titles in show conformation, proving that the hunting Chesapeake was also the ultimate example of the ideal standard for the breed.

Those years also saw the Chesapeake competing successfully in the breed and obedience rings, with many gaining bench (show) championships as well as CD (Companion Dog) and other obedience titles. Over 5,000 Chesapeakes were registered annually with the AKC. Although ranking behind its Labrador and Golden cousins, the Chessie still has a stronghold in the US today, with annual registrations around 4,500 and higher in recent years.

ACROSS THE ATLANTIC

As an all-American breed of dog, the Chesapeake Bay Retriever was slow gaining a foothold on other continents. Quarantines were undeniably an issue in the import of dogs to the United Kingdom and other European countries. American servicemen stationed in England during the war occasionally took their dogs through quarantine, with those dogs producing a few random litters. Serious efforts to introduce the breed rested with just a few dedicated individuals during the 1960s and 1970s.

In England, noted Flat-Coated Retriever breeder Margaret Izzard of Ryshot Kennels obtained her first Chesapeake in 1967 from breeder Mr. Bruce Kennedy, a cattleman from Scotland. Kennedy's litter was out of an American import named Doonholme Dusty, and Mrs. Izzard named her male pup Ryshot Welcome Yank, after his American roots. A strong proponent of the working dog, Mrs. Izzard worked Yank in the field with her Flat-Coated Retrievers, and Yank was always in demand at shoots on coastal estates where water work was difficult.

Looking for a mate for Yank, Mrs. Izzard imported Eastern Waters' Ryshot Rose from the US, and the two dogs were bred in 1974. From that breeding came Ryshot Yank's Sea Star, who went on to become the foundation bitch for Arnac Kennels, owned by the Lady Spencer-Smith. Yank's second breeding was in 1975 to the American import Eastern

---

A MULTI-TITLED GYPSY CLIPPER

Dual Ch. AFC Coot's Gypsy Clipper MH, bred by Carol Anderson and owned by Dr. Tom Ivey, was the first Chesapeake to earn all four of those AKC titles, each representing the top accomplishment in his area of expertise. The Dual Champion title refers to the show ring and field trials, the AFC refers to Amateur Field Champion and the MH refers to Master Hunter.

Waters' Morac, owned by Mr. J.H.A. Allen of Devonshire, England. Some of these pups and others from the Rose litter were exported to France, Sweden, Denmark and Finland to launch the breed in those countries.

After the death of Mrs. Izzard in 1975, few Chesapeake kennels remained in operation in the UK by 1977. About that time, breed fancier Sandy Hastings launched her Chesabay Kennel with an Arnac bitch puppy named Arnac Bay Abbey. Two years later, in 1979, Arnac Bay Beck, a sister to Abbey, was purchased by Janet Morris of Wales as the foundation bitch for her Penrose Kennels. Both Abbey and Beck competed on the bench and also worked in the field, and Abbey was the first Chesapeake to run a British field trial in 1979. Although Labradors still dominated in the field-trial circuit, winning most awards, Chesapeakes were quite successful in the working tests.

Although more Chesapeakes were being shown on the bench during the 1970s, the major awards still went to other Gundog breeds (equivalent to the AKC's Sporting Group). That changed in 1982, when the import Chestnut Hills Arnac Drake was shown at the United Retriever Club show, his first time on the bench since his release from quarantine. Drake not only won Best of Breed and Best Puppy in Breed at that first

show but also went on to be awarded Best in Show and Best Puppy in Show over the 300 dogs entered. Drake's success helped change the course of Chesapeakes in the ring in the UK.

By the following year, Chesapeake fanciers had mobilized and joined together to form a club to preserve the breed's legacy as a dual-purpose retriever and to organize shows and working tests to promote that end. Lady Spencer-Smith, together with Janet Morris and Joyce Munday, founded the Chesapeake Bay Retriever Club of the United Kingdom. Thereafter several new kennels emerged, with many using Arnac dogs as their foundation stock.

In 1984, the club held its first event, offering bench competition with working tests on the following day, and a record number of Chesapeakes entered on both days. Penrose Bronson, sired by the record-setting Chestnut Hills Arnac Drake and owned by Bruce Gauntlett, captured the Best in Show award, winning over her illustrious sire, who took Best of Opposite Sex.

Until that time, no Chesapeake had won a major field-trial award in the UK. The year 1984 broke new ground for the Chessie as a working breed when Janet Morris and her sedge bitch, Arnac Bay Dawnflight of

Penrose, took third place at a Novice any-variety licensed field trial. So historic was Dawn's accomplishment that a photograph of Dawn and Janet was published in an issue of the magazine *Shooting Times*. That same year witnessed more achievements for the Chesapeake in retriever working trials. Sharland Coxswain, bred by Joyce Munday and owned by Alan Cox, scored a win in a Puppy Dog stake, which was normally reserved only for professional handlers. Two such accomplishments in one year contributed mightily to a surge in interest in the breed.

The decade of the 1980s was indeed a productive one for the Chesapeake. More field-trial awards were captured in 1985 by the Arnac Bay and Penrose Kennels, with Lady Spencer-Smith's Arnac Bay Delta and Janet Morris's Penrose of Gunstock winning several ribbons. Janet Morris also scored again in the breed ring when Arnac Bay Beck of Penrose went on to Best in Show.

The following year, Arnac Bay Endurance, a full brother to the winning Dawn and her sister Delta, was handled to a field-trial win by his owner, Mr. John Barker. Endurance also sired Chesepi Amigo Mio, bred by Barker, and Penrose Eclipse, owned by Janet Morris, both of

This handsome English Chesapeake Bay Retriever from the 1930s was a winner in the Derby Stake. Ring, as he was known, was an excellent example of the Chessie in the UK during that period.

whom won field-trial awards in 1988. That same year, the breed further advanced as a dual-purpose dog when Lady Spencer-Smith's field-trial winner, Delta, also won on the bench at the club show.

During this decade, the focus on breed versatility had attracted several prominent fanciers from other breeds. Irish Water Spaniel breeder Elaine Griffin succumbed to the Chessie and took Penrose Delaware Dimbat of Tyheolog on to win the club show in 1987. Doberman Pinscher breeder Linda Partridge purchased Chesabay Coral of Braidenvale as a working field dog from breeder Sandy Hastings. In 1989, the pair went on to make breed history when they won a Novice any-variety retriever trial, besting a field dominated by Labradors and Golden Retrievers.

Linda and Coral were not finished writing new chapters in breed history, however. Three years later, they shocked the retriever world by winning an Open field trial, which is the most prestigious competitive event in the British retriever world. Coral's win capped a previous coup for the dual-purpose Chesapeake since Coral's sister, Chesabay Crystal of Arnac, had won Best of Breed at Crufts in 1992.

Until 1990, Crufts had limited the Chesapeake Bay Retriever to a group of imported breeds under

The Chessie in the US and beyond has garnered top prizes in field trials as well as in the show ring, demonstrating the breed's unique versatility and trainability.

Any Variety Not Separately Classified (AVNSC). On the first outing in their own class, field-trial award winner Chesepi Amigo Mio cemented the breed's dual-purpose status by winning Best of Breed. The versatile Arnac Bay Delta followed suit and handily took Best of Opposite Sex.

The working ability of the Chesapeake continues as the highest priority of Chesapeake breeders in Britain. Few breed specimens are shown in confor-mation, which breeders consider an important indication that greater interest lies with the working aspect of the breed.

Outside the UK, the breed has limited popularity in Europe. There are few Chesapeakes in Germany, where the breed is considered somewhat of a rarity. Through the early 1990s, there were about a dozen Chessies in the country, due primarily to the breeding of the superb English import, German-Swiss-Luxembourg Ch. Gunstock Brown Bosun, owned by Audrey Austin, to American import Holiday Surprise, owned by Karen Von Low. Their offspring became active in all areas of the dog sport, excelling in show, field and obedience.

In France, the Chesapeake remains a most uncommon breed, no doubt due to the many fine hunting breeds that originated in that country. Breed specimens in France are used primarily for hunting purposes on private estates, and the general public has little knowledge of the breed or its usefulness.

Mr. Phillippe Valette, an ardent French duck hunter, has bred, owned and hunted over Chesapeakes on his estate for over 40 years. Mr. Valette holds the breed in highest regard and tells of working in hunting parties who knocked down over 500 ducks a day. When the other retriever breeds fell tired and gave up, his Chesapeakes kept working until the last bird had been retrieved.

During the late 1990s, growing interest in the Chessie has brought several imports into France from Britain, the US and the Nether-lands. French fanciers are optimistic about the future of the breed in their country, which has long prized excellence in gundogs.

While the US has welcomed dozens of British breeds to its shores, the Chesapeake breed represents one of the few American breeds that has been accepted enthusiastically in Great Britain. The Australian Shep-herd and the Alaskan Mala-mute are two other examples.

An active all-American breed, the Chessie requires an enthusiastic, outdoor-loving owner in order to be happy and healthy. Are you read to take the lead and become a Chessie's life-long pal?

CHARACTERISTICS OF THE

CHESAPEAKE BAY RETRIEVER

The Chesapeake Bay Retriever has always been considered the paragon of duck dogs, the ultimate example of loyalty and courage, and has traditionally been the only logical choice for the true waterfowl enthusiast. As a family companion, he is both playmate and guardian of the children. Although trustworthy, he will not tolerate abuse and will get up and leave in such situations. Adult supervision is recommended during any child-dog interaction, indeed a wise precaution with dogs of any breed.

The Chesapeake is also protective of his home turf and can be trusted to protect the family property. Although he makes an excellent watchdog, he is a poor attack dog as he is not naturally inclined to inflict injury or harm. Those Chesapeakes who are known to be overly aggressive have unfortunately been irresponsibly bred or trained to be so, which is a true injustice to the breed. Chesapeake character has been affectionately described in historical literature as "...kind and gentle, a child can handle him; his heart knows no fear; he will stand

to his death in defense of his masters' person or property; on the bleakest shore on the coldest night, if a gun or coat is accidentally left, he will guard it."

Although the breed is possessed of an intense and affectionate personality, the Chesapeake is not fawning as are some other retriever breeds and tends to be standoffish with strangers. He is extremely intelligent and seems quite able to reason both when hunting in the field and in everyday life at home. On the negative side, as experienced owners frequently contend, he can be stubborn and irascible, and will resist training if he is unhappy with his situation or his owner. His attitude is often aloof and impassive during training, which makes him rather difficult to read, and he needs sustained authority if he is to learn and perform as directed.

A Chesapeake must receive consistent training while still a puppy if he is to fulfill his maximum potential and become a respectful member of the family and/or a responsive hunting partner. The owner must imprint all of the rules very early on his Chessie puppy's mind to mold the dog into a pleasant and obedient companion.

Despite his understated and somewhat passive personality, the Chesapeake lives best when part of his human family. He will accept confinement or kennel life, but will not thrive in a solitary state without people, as he absolutely requires love and a close association with his family. The Chesapeake is as serious about his work and responsibility to his family as he is to his role of hunter. He offers unsurpassed loyalty and devotion if his owner is firm, but, most importantly, also fair, loving and understanding.

OWNING A CHESAPEAKE BAY RETRIEVER

Although the Chesapeake has many fine qualities that you may find charming and appealing, this is not a breed for the typical inexperienced dog fancier. You should think seriously about why you want a dog and what you expect before adding one to your family.

A Chesapeake is not a wavy version of a Labrador or Golden Retriever; they are each very distinct breeds with completely different personalities. Bred originally as hard-working ducking dogs, Chessies still retain that original toughness required for working under severe hunting conditions. Intensely loyal,

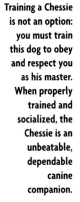

Training a Chessie is not an option: you must train this dog to obey and respect you as his master. When properly trained and socialized, the Chessie is an unbeatable, dependable canine companion.

serious and protective, they do not share the "love-everyone" attitude of other retriever breeds.

Basic training is not optional with a Chesapeake; it is essential if he is to respect you as his master and obey even the simplest of household rules. You must start his training when he is still a puppy, since that early imprinting is most important to his acceptance of you as his leader. Owners are wise to plan a minimum of eight to ten weeks of basic puppy school, where owner and pup learn to work together, supplemented by daily training sessions at home.

The Chesapeake will grow into a large, powerful and assertive dog, so growing up with rules he understands is a key element in successful cohabitation. If you are unassertive or unable to establish yourself as the leader or alpha person in his life, the dog will assume that role and make his own rules. Even a mild-mannered Chesapeake can become a dominant force who will intimidate family members whom he does not respect.

The sportsman who acquires a Chesapeake as a hunting partner also faces the same problems and challenges. A working Chessie must learn rules early in his life, receive firm, but fair and consistent, training and live within the family circle. Compatibility as a home companion is essential to

LIKE A PUP TO WATER...
Although the Chesapeake is a superb natural swimmer, you should use good sense when introducing a Chessie pup to water. Never throw him in, as that could cause a permanent fear of water. Use common sense and select a safe, calm, shallow area to entice the pup into the water.

successes in the field and duck blind.

The Chesapeake seldom offers exuberant displays of affection or frivolous, comical behavior. Although he enjoys petting and conversation and is emotionally sensitive to his master's moods, he is not overbearing or pushy and is content just to be nearby, simply sharing quiet time together.

DO YOU KNOW ABOUT HIP DYSPLASIA?

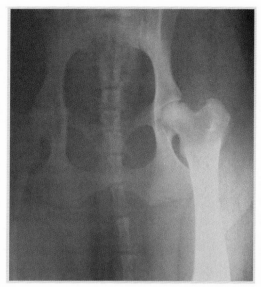

X-ray of a dog with "Good" hips.

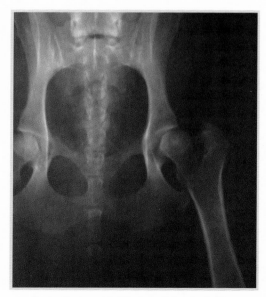

X-ray of a dog with "Moderate" dysplastic hips.

Hip dysplasia is a fairly common condition found in pure-bred dogs. When a dog has hip dysplasia, his hind leg has an incorrectly formed hip joint. By constant use of the hip joint, it becomes more and more loose, wears abnormally and may become arthritic.

Hip dysplasia can only be confirmed with an x-ray, but certain symptoms may indicate a problem. Your dog may have a hip dysplasia problem if he walks in a peculiar manner, hops instead of smoothly runs, uses his hind legs in unison (to keep the pressure off the weak joint), has trouble getting up from a prone position or always sits with both legs together on one side of his body.

As the dog matures, he may adapt well to life with a bad hip, but in a few years the arthritis develops and many dogs with hip dysplasia become crippled.

Hip dysplasia is considered an inherited disease and only can be diagnosed definitively by x-ray when the dog is two years old, although symptoms often appear earlier. Some experts claim that a special diet might help your puppy outgrow the bad hip, but the usual treatments are surgical. The removal of the pectineus muscle, the removal of the round part of the femur, reconstructing the pelvis and replacing the hip with an artificial one are all surgical interventions that are expensive, but they are usually very successful. Follow the advice of your veterinarian.

Conversely, he is also a working dog that requires daily physical exercise to maintain general health and muscle tone. As an active sporting dog bred for hard work, he will thrive on a daily regimen of activity—work, training or retrieving. Water work is his specialty, thus frequent swimming sessions will keep him healthy as well as content.

The Chesapeake is not the ideal breed for fussy house-keepers. This dog's intense love of water, combined with his unique, water-repellent coat, will result in large deposits of mud and grime indoors. Although the breed does not carry a long coat that requires professional grooming, Chessies do shed their undercoat twice yearly, sending clouds of "doggy down" all about the house.

HEALTH CONCERNS IN THE CHESAPEAKE

Every breed of pure-bred dog suffers from some hereditary diseases of which new owners should be aware. The Chessie is not excluded, though the breed is not as plagued by these genetic demons as many other working dogs. The following discussions are intended to apprise future owners of the specific conditions that can occur in the Chesapeake Bay Retriever, thus arming readers with questions and concerns to share with their chosen breeders.

HIP DYSPLASIA (HD)

Hip dysplasia is a hereditary disease that involves poor or abnormal formation of the hip joint. The disease affects many large breeds of dog, and Chesapeakes are no exception. A mild case of HD can cause painful arthritis in the average house dog, and a severe case can render a hunting dog worthless in the field. Diagnosis is made only through x-ray examination by a vet.

In the US, the Orthopedic Foundation for Animals (OFA) examines x-rays submitted for evaluation by vets across the

HIGH ACTIVITY
Like all retriever breeds, the Chesapeake is an active dog and will become destructive if he is bored or under-exercised. Your Chessie will let you know when he's tired, so never force exercise, as this can contribute to dysplastic problems. Likewise, don't overdo exercise with a developing pup.

Elbow dysplasia can only be diagnosed with an x-ray. This x-ray shows the dysplastic elbow of a three-and-a-half-year-old dog.

country. OFA rates the x-rays in six categories: Excellent, Good and Fair, which are the ratings required for breeding animals, and Mild, Moderate and Severe, ratings for dysplastic animals, which, of course, should not be bred.

Other countries have screening programs as well. The British Veterinary Association and Kennel Club (BVA/KC/HD) evaluate x-rays and assign a score of 0 (the best possible score) up to 53 (the worst possible score) for each hip, producing possible total scores of 0 to 106. Switzerland and Germany have strict rules; under their grading system, only dogs with grades of 0 or 1 are allowed to be bred, which has significantly reduced the incidence of HD in those countries.

Chesapeakes are very susceptible to HD, and all breeding stock should be x-rayed and certified at the requisite age (two years old in the US) before entering a breeding program.

ELBOW DYSPLASIA (ED) AND OSTEOCHONDRITIS DISSECANS (OCD)

Similar to HD that affects the joints of the hip, ED and OCD affect the joints of the elbow, shoulder, hock and stifle, with the shoulder and elbow the most commonly affected joints in most breeds. These diseases most often affect the growing joints of a large-

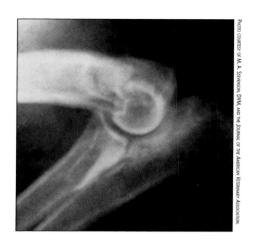

breed puppy under one year of age. An affected pup will usually exhibit symptoms between four and eight months of age, becoming lame for no apparent reason. Like HD, these conditions are only identified through x-ray, and surgery is often necessary to correct the problems.

Males are generally more predisposed than females, perhaps due to their more rapid rate of growth. These diseases tend to occur in certain families of dogs, with some lines showing higher incidences of the conditions. Environmental factors are also thought to play a role in the development of shoulder and elbow problems, with diet and excessive exercise heavily implicated as contributing factors.

EYE PROBLEMS

Chesapeakes are susceptible to progressive retinal atrophy (PRA), a progressive condition that eventually leads to blindness. Although the disease is inherited, affected dogs sometimes do not exhibit symptoms until four or five years of age. Dogs may be cleared for breeding after two years of age, but should be examined annually until eight years of age. Clearances must be obtained from a board-certified veterinary ophthalmologist.

If you obtain your Chessie puppy from a reputable breeder who has conducted the proper screening for hereditary concerns, you are ensured of a sound, healthy pup who will grow up to lead a productive, happy life with his new family.

CHESAPEAKE BAY RETRIEVER

The *type* of each breed of dog is guided by that breed's standard, which is a blueprint or road map of sorts that outlines the breed's ideal physical properties and temperament, and the abilities necessary for the task for which the dog was intended. Standards are written by knowledgeable breed experts who hope to ensure the quality of a particular breed for future generations. Without such guidelines, specific inherent breed characteristics may be altered or completely eliminated.

The parent club drafts the standard and the American Kennel Club (AKC) approves it. In the Chesapeake Bay Retriever, coat and color are essential characteristics of the breed. From the earliest descriptions of the Chesapeake Bay Ducking Dog, both were of primary consideration. The oily outer coat and woolly undercoat were essential to the dog's working in harsh weather conditions.

Early colors were identified as a blending of different hues, resembling in its variations the reddish-brown mud and clay shores of the Chesapeake Bay and its tributaries. In certain parts of the Bay, breeders worked for a deadgrass or sedge color to match the autumn and winter coloring of the marshes. Thus, every facet of coloring in the Chessie has its origin in the desire of those original breeders to perfect a camouflage for a dog whose color was chosen to blend with his surroundings. Indeed, the requirements set forth in the standard emphasize the extreme importance of correct coat and color.

THE AMERICAN KENNEL CLUB STANDARD FOR THE CHESAPEAKE BAY RETRIEVER

GENERAL APPEARANCE

Equally proficient on land and in the water, the Chesapeake Bay Retriever was developed along the Chesapeake Bay to hunt waterfowl under the most adverse weather and water conditions, often having to break ice during the course of many strenuous multiple retrieves.

SWIMMER'S REAR
Because the Chesapeake is a swimming dog, he is known for his powerful hindquarters, which are as high or a bit higher than his shoulders.

Frequently the Chesapeake must face wind, tide and long cold swims in its work. The breed's characteristics are specifically suited to enable the Chesapeake to function with ease, efficiency and endurance. In head, the Chesapeake's skull is broad and round with a medium stop. The jaws should be of sufficient length and strength to carry large game birds with an easy, tender hold. The double coat consists of a short, harsh, wavy outer coat and a dense, fine, woolly undercoat containing an abundance of natural oil and is ideally suited for the icy rugged conditions of weather the Chesapeake often works in. In body, the Chesapeake is a strong, well-balanced, powerfully built animal of moderate size and medium length in body and leg, deep and wide in chest, the shoulders built with full liberty of movement, and with no tendency to weakness in any feature, particularly the rear. The power though, should not be at the expense of agility or stamina. Size and substance should not be excessive as this is a working retriever of an active nature.

Distinctive features include eyes that are very clear, of yellowish or amber hue, hindquarters as high or a trifle higher than the shoulders, and a double coat which tends to wave on shoulders, neck, back and loins only.

The Chesapeake is valued for its bright and happy disposition, intelligence, quiet good sense, and affectionate protective nature. Extreme shyness or extreme aggressive tendencies are not desirable in the breed either as a gun dog or companion. *Disqualifications*: Specimens that are lacking in breed characteristics should be disqualified.

SIZE, PROPORTION, SUBSTANCE

Height—Males should measure 23 to 26 inches; females should measure 21 to 24 inches. Oversized or undersized animals are to be severely penalized. Proportion— Height from the top of the shoulder blades to the ground should be slightly less than the body length from the breastbone to the point of buttocks. Depth of

When Chesapeake Bay Retrievers are exhibited at dog shows, the judge uses the breed standard to determine which dog most closely conforms to this written description of the ideal for the breed. This important document is the barometer by which judges and breeders assess the quality of a given dog.

A correct head in profile.

preferred, but a level bite is acceptable. *Disqualifications*: Either undershot or overshot bites are to be disqualified.

NECK, TOPLINE, BODY

Neck should be of medium length with a strong muscular appearance, tapering to the shoulders. Topline should show the hindquarters to be as high as or a trifle higher than the shoulders. Back should be short, well coupled and powerful. Chest should be strong, deep and wide. Rib cage barrel round and deep. Body is of medium length, neither cobby nor roached, but rather approaching hollowness from underneath as the flanks should be well tucked up. Tail of medium length; medium heavy at the base. The tail should be straight or slightly curved and should not curl over back or side kink.

body should extend at least to the elbow. Shoulder to elbow and elbow to ground should be equal. Weight—Males should weigh 65 to 80 pounds; females should weigh 55 to 70 pounds.

HEAD

The Chesapeake Bay Retriever should have an intelligent expression. Eyes are to be medium large, very clear, of yellowish or amber color and wide apart. Ears are to be small, set well up on the head, hanging loosely, and of medium leather. Skull is broad and round with a medium stop. Nose is medium short. Muzzle is approximately the same length as the skull, tapered, pointed but not sharp. Lips are thin, not pendulous. Bite—Scissors is

FOREQUARTERS

There should be no tendency to weakness in the forequarters. Shoulders should be sloping with full liberty of action, plenty of power and without any restrictions of movement. Legs should be

ABOUT THE COAT
The unique quality of the Chesapeake's coat allows the dog to go from the field into the show ring on the same day without the embellishments necessary in other breeds of dog.

IMPORTANCE OF COLOR

In most pure-bred dogs, color is rarely a consideration beyond the mere esthetics of conformation. In the Chessie, the desired deadgrass color has more to do with function than beauty. The proper hue of deadgrass camouflages the dog along the banks of the Bay, thus making him a more efficient hunter.

medium in length and straight, showing good bone and muscle. Pasterns slightly bent and of medium length. The front legs should appear straight when viewed from front or rear. Dewclaws on the forelegs may be removed. Well webbed hare feet should be of good size with toes well-rounded and close.

HINDQUARTERS

Good hindquarters are essential. They should show fully as much power as the forequarters. There should be no tendency to weakness in the hindquarters. Hindquarters should be especially powerful to supply the driving power for swimming. Legs should be medium length and straight, showing good bone and muscle. Stifles should be well angulated. The distance from hock to ground should be of medium length. The hind legs should look straight when viewed from the front or rear. Dewclaws, if any, must be removed from the hind legs. *Disqualifications:* Dewclaws on the hind legs are a disqualification.

COAT

Coat should be thick and short, nowhere over 1.5 inches long, with a dense fine woolly undercoat. Hair on the face and legs should be very short and straight with a tendency to wave on the shoulders, neck, back and loins only. Moderate feathering on rear of hindquarters and tail is permissible.

The texture of the Chesapeake's coat is very important, as the Chesapeake is used for hunting under all sorts of adverse weather conditions, often working in ice and snow. The oil in the harsh outer coat and woolly undercoat is of extreme value in preventing the cold water from reaching the Chesapeake's skin and aids in

Dog in profile showing the correct substance, balance, type and coat.

The colors of the breed are described as brown, sedge and deadgrass, illustrated in these three dogs, from left to right.

quick drying. A Chesapeake's coat should resist the water in the same way that a duck's feathers do. When the Chesapeake leaves the water and shakes, the coat should not hold water at all, being merely moist.

Disqualifications: A coat that is curly or has a tendency to curl all over the body must be disqualified. Feathering on the tail or legs over 1.75 inches long must be disqualified.

COLOR

The color of the Chesapeake Bay Retriever must be as nearly that of its working surroundings as possible. Any color of brown, sedge or deadgrass is acceptable, self-colored Chesapeakes being preferred. One color is not to be preferred over another. A white spot on the breast, belly, toes, or back of the feet (immediately above the large pad) is permissible, but the smaller the spot the better, solid colored preferred. The color of the coat and its texture must be given every consideration when judging on the bench or in the ring. Honorable scars are not to be penalized. *Disqualifications:* Black colored; white on any part of the body except breast, belly, toes, or back of feet must be disqualified.

GAIT

The gait should be smooth, free and effortless, giving the impression of great power and strength. When viewed from the side, there should be good reach with no restrictions of movement in the front and plenty of drive in the rear, with good flexion of the stifle and hock joints. Coming at you, there should be no sign of elbows

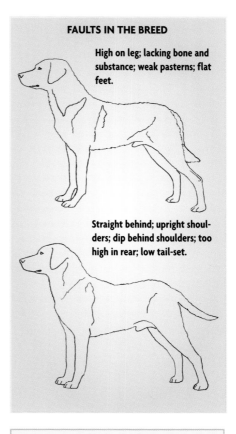

FAULTS IN THE BREED

High on leg; lacking bone and substance; weak pasterns; flat feet.

Straight behind; upright shoulders; dip behind shoulders; too high in rear; low tail-set.

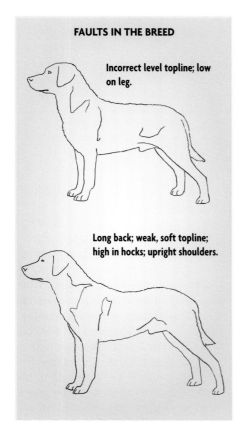

FAULTS IN THE BREED

Incorrect level topline; low on leg.

Long back; weak, soft topline; high in hocks; upright shoulders.

BEWARE THE LONG HAIR

Although long-hair genes are fairly rare in most lines of Chesapeakes, longhaired pups still occasionally occur. A longhaired Chesapeake is defined as any Chessie that has a coat longer than what is called for in the standard, tail furnishings excepted. Long hair is considered a simple recessive gene and is a disqualification in the breed. The long-hair gene may be due to crosses with generic spaniel types and other water dogs.

being out. When the Chesapeake is moving away from you, there should be no sign of cowhockness from the rear. As speed increases, the feet tend to converge toward a center line of gravity.

TEMPERAMENT

The Chesapeake Bay Retriever should show a bright and happy disposition with an intelligent expression. Courage, willingness to work, alertness, nose, intelligence, love of water, general quality and, most of all, disposition should be given primary consideration in the selection and breeding of the Chesapeake Bay Retriever.

DISQUALIFICATIONS

1. Specimens lacking in breed characteristics.
2. Teeth overshot or undershot.
3. Dewclaws on the hind legs.
4. Coat curly or with a tendency to curl all over the body.
5. Feathering on the tail or legs over 1.75 inches long.
6. Black colored.
7. White on any part of the body except breast, belly, toes, or back of feet.

The question of coat and general type of balance takes precedence over any scoring table which could be drawn up. The Chesapeake should be well proportioned, an animal with a good coat and well balanced in other points being preferable to one excelling in some but weak in others.

POSITIVE SCALE OF POINTS

Head (including lips, ears and eyes)	16
Neck	4
Shoulders and body	12
Hindquarters and stifles	12
Elbows, legs and feet	12
Color	4
Stern and tail	10
Coat and texture	18
General conformation	12
TOTAL	**100**

APPROXIMATE MEASUREMENT

	INCHES
• Length head, nose to occiput	9.5 to 10
• Girth at ears	20 to 21
• Muzzle below eyes	10 to 10.5
• Length of ears	4.5 to 5
• Width between eyes	2.5 to 2.75
• Girth neck close to shoulder	20 to 22
• Girth at flank	24 to 25
• Length from occiput to tail base	34 to 35
• Girth forearms at shoulders	10 to 10.5
• Girth upper thigh	19 to 20
• From root to root of ear, over skull	5 to 6
• Occiput to top shoulder blades	9 to 9.5
• From elbow to elbow over the shoulders	25 to 26

Approved November 9, 1993
Effective December 31, 1993

CHESAPEAKE BAY RETRIEVER

SELECTING A CHESAPEAKE BAY PUPPY

The key to finding a quality Chesapeake puppy is finding a reputable breeder who produces sound, healthy, typical pups. Responsible breeders use only sound representatives of the breed in their breeding programs and always screen their breeding stock for genetic diseases.

Health and temperament are the primary concerns when selecting a pup of any breed. You should look for a stable pleasant temperament, with no hint of shyness, fear or aggression. Pups should be unruffled by loud or sudden noises and be eager to approach strangers. They should be active and energetic and should be retrieving items with eagerness. Pups should have glossy coats, bright eyes and healthy pink gums.

Puppy and adult coat colors can range from a very light dead-grass to a dark, rich chocolate shade. You can find a wide range of colors within the same litter. A Chesapeake puppy's coat color may become darker or lighter with maturity.

Chessie puppies are irresistible, but remember to follow your head and not just your heart when visiting a litter. You must select a well-bred, healthy puppy from an above-average sire and dam.

The sire and dam should be certified as free of hip and elbow dysplasia and be currently certified as free of eye disease, showing that their eyes are tested yearly. Look closely at the parents of the pup, as they will reflect the qualities passed along to their get. The dam should be on the premises and, if the sire is not, you should at least see a photo. If you don't like the parents, you should look elsewhere for a puppy.

research and found a responsible, conscientious person who breeds quality Chessies and who should become a reliable source of help as you and your puppy adjust to life together. If you have observed a litter in action, you have obtained a firsthand look at the dynamics of a puppy "pack" and,

You can determine much about your future pup's appearance and temperament by meeting one of the parents.

Final puppy selection should be determined by your goals for your dog. If you are looking for a hunting partner, you should check for field titles in the pedigree well before committing to a pup; if none is present, you should observe the parents working in the field to determine if they are capable hunting dogs. If you have aspirations in the show ring or obedience, look for corresponding titles in the pedigree.

COMMITMENT OF OWNERSHIP

After considering these factors, you have most likely already made some very important decisions about selecting your puppy. You have chosen the Chesapeake Bay Retriever, which means that you have decided which characteristics you want in a dog and what type of dog will best fit into your family and lifestyle. If you have selected a breeder, you have gone a step further—you have done your

PEDIGREE VS. REGISTRATION CERTIFICATE

Too often new owners are confused between these two important documents. Your puppy's pedigree, essentially a family tree, is a written record of a dog's genealogy of three generations or more. The pedigree will show you the names as well as performance titles of all dogs in your pup's background. Your breeder must provide you with a registration application, with his part properly filled out. You must complete the application and send it to the AKC with the proper fee. Every puppy must come from a litter that has been AKC-registered by the breeder, born in the USA and from a sire and dam that are also registered with the AKC.

The seller must provide you with complete records to identify the puppy. The AKC requires that the seller provide the buyer with the following: breed; sex, color and markings; date of birth; litter number (when available); names and registration numbers of the parents; breeder's name; and date sold or delivered.

thus, you have learned about each pup's individual personality—perhaps you have even found one that particularly appeals to you.

However, even if you have not yet found the Chesapeake puppy of your dreams, observing pups will help you learn to recognize certain behavior and to determine what a pup's behavior indicates about his temperament. You will be able to pick out which pups are the leaders, which ones are less outgoing, which ones are confident, shy, playful, friendly, etc. Equally as important, you will learn to recognize what a healthy pup should look and act like. All of these things will help you in your search, and when you find the Chessie that was meant for you, you'll know it!

Researching your breed, selecting a responsible breeder and observing as many pups as possible are all important steps on the way to dog ownership. It may seem like a lot of effort...and you have not even taken the pup home yet! Remember, though, you cannot be too careful when it comes to deciding on the type of dog you want and finding out about your prospective pup's background. Buying a puppy is not—or *should* not be—just a whimsical purchase. This is one instance in which you actually do get to choose your own family! You may be thinking that buying a puppy should be fun—it should

ARE YOU PREPARED?

Unfortunately, when a puppy is bought by someone who does not take into consideration the time and attention that dog ownership requires, it is the puppy who suffers when he is either abandoned or placed in a shelter by a frustrated owner. So all of the "homework" you do in preparation for your pup's arrival will benefit you both. The more informed you are, the more you will know what to expect and the better equipped you will be to handle the ups and downs of raising a puppy. Hopefully, everyone in the household is willing to do his part in raising and caring for the pup. The anticipation of owning a dog often brings a lot of promises from excited family members: "I will walk him every day," "I will feed him," "I will house-train him," etc., but these things take time and effort, and promises can easily be forgotten once the novelty of the new pet has worn off.

not be so serious and so much work. Keep in mind that your puppy is not a cuddly stuffed toy or decorative lawn ornament; rather, he is a living creature that will become a real member of your family. You will come to realize that, while buying a puppy is a pleasurable and exciting endeavor, it is not something to be taken lightly. Relax...the fun will start when the pup comes home!

Always keep in mind that a puppy is nothing more than a baby in a furry disguise...a baby who is virtually helpless in a human world and who trusts his owner for fulfillment of his basic needs for survival. In addition to food, water and shelter, your pup needs care, protection, guidance and love. If you are not prepared to commit to this, then you are not prepared to own a dog.

"Wait a minute," you say. "How hard could this be? All of my neighbors own dogs and they seem to be doing just fine. Why should I have to worry about all of this?" Well, you should not worry about it; in fact, you will probably find that once your Chesapeake pup gets used to his new home, he will fall into his place in the family quite naturally. However, it never hurts to emphasize the

The Chessie rainbow! From left to right, pups in shades of brown, sedge and deadgrass.

commitment of dog ownership. With some time and patience, it is really not too difficult to raise a curious and exuberant Chesapeake pup to become a well-adjusted and well-mannered adult dog—a dog that could be your most loyal friend.

PREPARING PUPPY'S PLACE IN YOUR HOME

Researching your breed and finding a breeder are only two aspects of the "homework" you will have to do before taking your Chesapeake puppy home. You will also have to prepare your home and family for the new addition. Much as you would prepare a nursery for a newborn baby, you will need to designate a place in your home that will be the puppy's own. How you prepare your home will depend on how much freedom the dog will be allowed. Whatever you decide, you must ensure that he has a place that he can call his own.

When you bring your new puppy into your home, you are bringing him into what will become his home as well. Obviously, you did not buy a puppy with the intentions of catering to his every whim and allowing him to "rule the roost," but in order for a puppy to grow into a stable, well-adjusted dog, he has to feel comfortable in his surroundings. Remember, he is

YOUR SCHEDULE...
If you lead an erratic, unpredictable life, with daily or weekly changes in your work requirements, consider the problems of owning a puppy. The new puppy has to be fed regularly, socialized (loved, petted, handled, introduced to other people) and, most importantly, allowed to go outdoors for house-training. As the dog gets older, he can be more tolerant of deviations in his feeding and relief schedule.

leaving the warmth and security of his mother and littermates, as well as the familiarity of the only place he has ever known, so it is important to make his transition as easy as possible. By preparing a place in your home for the puppy, you are making him feel as welcome as possible in a strange new place. It should not take him long to get used to it, but the sudden shock of being transplanted is somewhat traumatic for a young pup. Imagine how a small child would feel in the same situation—that is how your puppy

You can count on your new Chessie to bring much joy and excitement into your family's life. Along with the fun comes the responsibility of each family member to put time and effort into raising the pup.

> ## "YOU BETTER SHOP AROUND!"
> Finding a reputable breeder who sells healthy pups is very important, but make sure that the breeder you choose is not only someone you respect but also someone with whom you feel comfortable. Your breeder will be a resource long after you buy your puppy, and you must be able to call with reasonable questions without being made to feel like a pest! If you don't connect on a personal level, investigate some other breeders before making a final decision. Likewise, the breeder will ask you a lot of questions to ensure that you'll be a fit owner for his puppy.

must be feeling. It is up to you to reassure him and to let him know, "Little duck dog, you are going to like it here!"

WHAT YOU SHOULD BUY

CRATE
To someone unfamiliar with the use of crates in dog training, it may seem like punishment to shut a dog in a crate, but this is not the case at all. Although all breeders do not advocate crate training, more and more breeders and trainers are recommending crates as preferred tools for pet puppies as well as show puppies.

Crates are not cruel—crates have many humane and highly

effective uses in dog care and training. For example, crate training is a very popular and very successful house-training method. In addition, a crate can keep your dog safe during travel and, perhaps most importantly, a crate provides your dog with a place of his own in your home. It serves as a "doggie bedroom" of sorts—your Chesapeake can curl up in his crate when he wants to sleep or when he just needs a break. Many dogs sleep in their crates overnight. With soft bedding and his favorite toy, a crate becomes a cozy pseudo-den for your dog. Like his ancestors, he too will seek out the comfort and retreat of a den—you just happen to be providing him with something far more luxurious than what his early ancestors enjoyed.

As far as purchasing a crate, the type that you buy is up to you. It will most likely be one of the two most popular types: wire or fiberglass. There are advantages and disadvantages to each type. For example, a wire crate is more open, allowing the air to flow through and affording the dog a view of what is going on around him, while a fiberglass crate is sturdier. Both can double as travel crates, providing protection for the dog in the car. The size of the crate is another thing to consider. Puppies do not stay puppies forever—in fact, sometimes it

PUPPY APPEARANCE

Your puppy should have a well-fed appearance but not a distended abdomen, which may indicate worms or incorrect feeding, or both. The body should be firm, with a solid feel. The skin of the abdomen should be pale pink and clean, without signs of scratching or rash. Check the hind legs to make certain that dewclaws were removed, if any were present at birth.

Your local pet shop should have a wide selection of crates. Get a large-sized crate, as your Chessie puppy will grow quickly and you want the crate to accommodate him as an adult.

seems as if they grow right before your eyes. A small crate may be fine for a very young Chesapeake pup, but it will not do him much good for long! Unless you have the money and the inclination to buy a new crate every time your pup has a growth spurt, it is better to get one that will accommodate your dog both as a pup and at full size. A large-sized crate will be

necessary for a fully-grown Chesapeake, who can stand as tall as 26 inches at the shoulder. The proper crate should measure at least 42 inches long by 28 inches wide by 32 inches high.

BEDDING

A soft lambswool pad in the dog's crate will help the dog feel more at home, and you may also like to give him a small blanket. First, this will take the place of the leaves, twigs, etc., that the pup would use in the wild to make a den; the pup can make his own "burrow" in the crate. Although your pup is far removed from his den-making ancestors, the denning instinct is still a part of his genetic makeup. Second, until you take your pup home, he has been sleeping amid the warmth of his mother and littermates, and while a blanket is not the same as a warm, breathing body, it still provides heat and something with which to snuggle. You will want to wash your pup's bedding frequently in case he has a potty accident in his crate, and replace or remove any blanket or padding that becomes ragged and starts to fall apart.

TOYS

Toys are a must for dogs of all ages, especially for curious playful pups. Puppies are the "children" of the dog world, and what child does not love toys?

Chew toys provide enjoyment for both dog and owner—your dog will enjoy playing with his favorite toys, while you will enjoy the fact that they distract him from chewing on your expensive shoes and leather sofa. Puppies love to chew; in fact, chewing is a physical need for pups as they are teething, and everything looks appetizing! The full range of your possessions—from old dishcloth to Oriental carpet—are fair game in the eyes of a teething pup. Puppies are not all that discerning when it comes to finding something literally to "sink their teeth into"—everything tastes great!

Chesapeake puppies are fairly aggressive chewers and only the hardest, strongest toys should be offered to them. Breeders advise owners to resist stuffed toys, because they can become de-stuffed in no time. The overly excited pup may ingest the stuffing, which is neither nutritious nor digestible.

Similarly, squeaky toys are quite popular, but must be avoided for the Chesapeake. Perhaps a squeaky toy can be used as an aid in training, but not for free play. If a pup "disembowels" one of these, the small plastic squeaker inside can be dangerous if swallowed. Monitor the condition of all your pup's toys carefully and get rid of any that have been chewed to the point of

CRATE-TRAINING TIPS

During crate training, you should partition off the section of the crate in which the pup stays. If he is given too big an area, this will hinder your training efforts. Crate training is based on the fact that a dog does not like to soil his sleeping quarters, so it is ineffective to keep a pup in an area that is so big that he can eliminate in one end and get far enough away from it to sleep. Also, you want to make the crate den-like for the pup. Blankets and a favorite toy will make the crate cozy for the small pup; as he grows, you may want to evict some of his "roommates" to make more room. It will take some coaxing at first, but be patient. Given some time to get used to it, your pup will adapt to his new home-within-a-home quite nicely.

Chessie pups may not necessary be the same color as their parents. Color is only a deciding factor if your Chessie is destined for hunting work. Otherwise, personal preference is all that matters, provided the pup is sound and healthy.

becoming potentially dangerous.

Be careful of natural bones, which have a tendency to splinter into sharp, dangerous pieces. Also be careful of rawhide, which can turn into pieces that are easy to swallow and become a mushy mess on your carpet.

LEAD

A nylon lead is probably the best option, as it is the most resistant to puppy teeth should your pup take a liking to chewing on his

TEETHING TIP

Puppies like soft toys for chewing. Because they are teething, soft items like stuffed toys soothe their aching gums, but be sure to monitor your pup when he's playing with a potentially destructible (and thus potentially dangerous) toy.

lead. Of course, this is a habit that should be nipped in the bud, but, if your pup likes to chew on his lead, he has a very slim chance of being able to chew through the strong nylon. Nylon leads are also lightweight, which is good for a young Chesapeake who is just getting used to the idea of walking on a lead. For everyday walking and safety purposes, the nylon lead is a good choice.

As your pup grows up and can walk on the lead politely, you may want to purchase a flexible lead. These leads allow you to extend the length to give the dog a broader area to explore or to shorten the length to keep the dog near you. These leads have weight limitations, so be sure your Chessie isn't too heavy for the lead. Of course, there are leads designed for training purposes and harnesses made for working dogs, but these are not necessary for routine walks.

COLLAR

Your pup should get used to wearing a collar all the time since you will want to attach his ID tags to it; plus, you have to attach the lead to something! A lightweight nylon collar is a good choice. Make certain that the collar fits snugly enough so that the pup cannot wriggle out of it, but is loose enough so that it will not be uncomfortably tight around the pup's neck. You should be able to

Your local pet shop should have a wide array of leads suitable for your Chessie.

TOYS, TOYS, TOYS!

With a big variety of dog toys available, and so many that look like they would be a lot of fun for a dog, be careful in your selection. It is amazing what a set of puppy teeth can do to an innocent-looking toy, so, obviously, safety is a major consideration. Be sure to choose the most durable products that you can find. Hard nylon bones and toys are a safe bet, and many of them are offered in different scents and flavors that will be sure to capture your dog's attention. It is always fun to play a game of fetch with your dog, and there are balls and flying discs that are specially made to withstand dog teeth.

fit a finger between the pup's neck and the collar. It may take some time for your pup to get used to wearing the collar, but soon he will not even notice that it is there. Choke collars are made for training, but should only be used by those who have been instructed in their proper use.

FOOD AND WATER BOWLS

Your pup will need two bowls, one for food and one for water. You may want two sets of bowls, one for indoors and one for outdoors, depending on where the dog will be fed and where he will be spending time. Stainless steel or sturdy plastic bowls are popular choices. Plastic bowls are

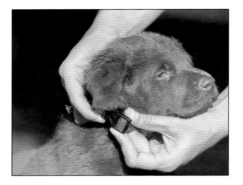

A simple nylon buckle collar makes a suitable choice for your Chessie pup's first collar because it can be adjusted as the pup grows.

more chewable, but dogs tend not to chew on the steel variety, which can be sterilized. It is important to buy sturdy bowls since anything is in danger of being chewed by puppy teeth and you do not want your dog to be constantly chewing apart his bowl (for his safety and for your

purse!). Stands on which to elevate the Chessie's bowls are strongly recommended, as this is a preventative measure against bloat. This potentially fatal condition affects many large, deep-chested breeds, including the Chessie.

CLEANING SUPPLIES

Until a pup is house-trained, you will be doing a lot of cleaning. "Accidents" will occur, which is acceptable in the beginning stages of toilet training because the puppy does not know any better. All you can do is be prepared to clean up any accidents as soon as they happen. Old rags, towels, newspapers and a safe disinfectant are good to have on hand.

Sturdy fencing should be in place before pup comes home.

CHOOSE AN APPROPRIATE COLLAR

The BUCKLE COLLAR is the standard collar used for everyday purposes. Be sure that you adjust the buckle on growing puppies. Check it every day. It can become too tight overnight! These collars can be made of leather or nylon. Attach your dog's identification tags to this collar.

The CHOKE COLLAR is designed for training. It is constructed of highly polished steel so that it slides easily through the stainless steel loop. The idea is that the dog controls the pressure around his neck and he will stop pulling if the collar becomes uncomfortable. It is used *only* for training and *never* left on a dog.

The HALTER is for a trained dog that has to be restrained to prevent running away, chasing a cat and the like. Considered the most humane of all collars, it is frequently used on smaller dogs on which collars are not comfortable.

Large, durable bowls and bowl stands are necessary tools for feeding your Chessie.

PHOTO COURTESY OF MIKKI PET PRODUCTS.

BEYOND THE BASICS

The items previously discussed are the bare necessities. You will find out what else you need as you go along—grooming supplies, flea/tick protection, baby gates to partition a room, etc. These things will vary depending on your situation, but it is important that right away you have everything you need to feed and make your Chessie comfortable in his first few days at home.

PUPPY-PROOFING YOUR HOME

Aside from making sure that your Chesapeake will be comfortable in your home, you also have to make sure that your home is safe for your Chesapeake. This means taking precautions that your pup will not get into anything he should not get into and that there is nothing within his reach that may harm him should he sniff it, chew it, inspect it, etc. This probably seems obvious since, while you are primarily con-cerned with your pup's safety, at the same time you do not want your belongings to be ruined. Breakables should be placed out of reach if your dog is to have full run of the house. If he is to be limited to certain places within the house, keep any potentially dangerous items in the "off-limits" areas.

An electrical cord can pose a danger should the puppy decide to taste it—and who is going to

It is your responsibility to clean up after your dog has relieved himself. Pet shops have various aids to assist in the cleanup job.

FEEDING TIPS

You will probably start feeding your pup the same food that he has been getting from the breeder; the breeder should give you a few days' supply to start you off. Although you should not give your pup too many treats, you will want to have puppy treats on hand for coaxing, training, rewards, etc. Be careful, though, as a small pup's calorie requirements are relatively low and a few treats can add up to almost a full day's worth of calories without the required nutrition.

convince a pup that it would not make a great chew toy? All cords and wires should be fastened tightly against the wall to keep them from puppy teeth. If your dog is going to spend time in a crate, make sure that there is nothing near his crate that he can reach if he sticks his curious little nose or paws through the openings. Just as you would with a child, keep all household cleaners and chemicals where the pup cannot reach them.

It is also important to make sure that the outside of your home is safe. Of course, your puppy should never be unsupervised, but a pup let loose in the yard will want to run and explore, and he

PLAY'S THE THING

Teaching the puppy to play with his toys in running and fetching games is an ideal way to help the puppy develop muscle, learn motor skills and bond with you, his owner and master. He also needs to learn how to inhibit his bite reflex and never to use his teeth on people, forbidden objects and other animals in play. Whenever you play with your puppy, you make the rules. This becomes an important message to your puppy in teaching him that you are the pack leader and control everything he does in life. Once your dog accepts you as his leader, your relationship with him will be cemented for life.

should be granted that freedom. Do not let a fence give you a false sense of security; you would be surprised at how crafty (and persistent) a dog can be in working out how to dig under and squeeze his way through small holes, or to jump or climb over a fence.

Chessies are more inclined to dig than to jump; nevertheless, always err on the side of caution where your pets are concerned. Make the fence well embedded into the ground and high enough so that it really is impossible for your dog to get over it (about 6 feet should suffice). Be sure to secure any gaps in the fence. Check the fence periodically to ensure that it is in good shape and make repairs as needed; a very determined pup may return to the same spot to "work on it" until he is able to get through.

FIRST TRIP TO THE VET

You have selected your puppy, and your home and family are ready. Now all you have to do is collect your Chesapeake from the breeder and the fun begins, right? Well…not so fast. Something else you need to plan is your pup's first trip to the veterinarian. Perhaps the breeder can recommend someone in the area who specializes in retriever breeds, or maybe you know some other Chessie owners who can suggest a good vet. Either way, you should have an appointment arranged for your pup before you pick him up.

The pup's first visit will consist of an overall examination to make sure that the pup does not have any problems that are not apparent to you. The veterinarian will also set up a schedule for the pup's vaccinations; the breeder will inform you of which ones the pup has already received and the vet can continue from there.

INTRODUCTION TO THE FAMILY

Everyone in the house will be excited about the puppy's coming home and will want to pet him and play with him, but it is best to make the introduction low-key so as not to overwhelm the puppy. He is apprehensive already. It is the first time he has been separated from his mother and the breeder, and the ride to your home is likely to be the first time he has been in a car. The last thing you want to do is smother him, as this will only frighten him further. This is not to say that human contact is not extremely necessary at this stage, because this is the time when a connection between the pup and his human family is formed. Gentle petting and soothing words should help console him, as well as just putting him down and letting him explore on his own (under your watchful eye, of course).

NATURAL TOXINS

Examine your grass and landscaping before bringing your puppy home. Many varieties of plants have leaves, stems or flowers that are toxic if ingested, and you can depend on a curious puppy to investigate them. Ask your vet for information on poisonous plants or research them at your library.

If you see your dog carrying a piece of vegetation in his mouth, approach him in a quiet, disinterested manner, avoid eye contact, pet him and gradually remove the plant from his mouth. Alternatively, offer him a treat and maybe he'll drop the plant on his own accord. Be sure no toxic plants are growing in your own yard or kept in your home.

Meeting the family cat will probably be more stressful for the cat than for your playful Chessie pup. Supervise all introductions so that your Chessie doesn't have a negative experience and grow up to fear or dislike the feline species.

The pup may approach the family members or may busy himself with exploring for a while. Gradually, each person should spend some time with the pup, one at a time, crouching down to get as close to the pup's level as possible while letting him sniff their hands and petting him gently. He definitely needs human attention and he needs to be touched—this is how to form an immediate bond. Just remember that the pup is experiencing many things for the first time, at the same time. There are new people, new noises, new smells and new things to investigate, so be gentle, be affectionate and be as comforting as you can be.

PUP'S FIRST NIGHT HOME

You have traveled home with your new charge safely in his crate. He's been to the vet for a thorough check-up; he's been weighed, his papers have been examined and perhaps he's even been vaccinated and wormed as well. He's met the whole family, including the excited children and the less-than-happy cat. He's explored his area, his new bed, the yard and anywhere else he's been permitted. He's eaten his first meal at home and relieved himself in the proper place. He's heard lots of new sounds, smelled new friends and seen more of the outside world than ever before… and that was just the first day! He's worn out and is ready for bed…or so you think!

It's puppy's first night home and you are ready to say "Good night." Keep in mind that this is his first night ever to be sleeping alone. His dam and littermates are no longer at paw's length and he's

SKULL & CROSSBONES

Thoroughly puppy-proof your house before bringing your puppy home. Never use cockroach or rodent poisons or plant fertilizers in any area accessible to the puppy. Avoid the use of toilet cleaners. Most dogs are born with "toilet-bowl sonar" and will take a drink if the lid is left open. Also keep the trash secured and out of reach.

a bit scared, cold and lonely. Be reassuring to your new family member, but this is not the time to spoil him and give in to his inevitable whining.

Puppies whine. They whine to let others know where they are and hopefully to get company out of it. Place your pup in his new bed or crate in his designated area and close the crate door. Mercifully, he may fall asleep without a peep. When the inevitable occurs, however, ignore the whining—he is fine. Be strong and keep his interest in mind. Do not allow yourself to feel guilty and visit the pup. He will fall asleep eventually.

Many breeders recommend placing a piece of bedding from the pup's former home in his new bed so that he recognizes and is comforted by the scent of his littermates. Others still advise placing a hot water bottle in the bed for warmth. The latter may be a good idea provided the pup doesn't attempt to suckle—he'll get good and wet and may not fall asleep so fast.

Puppy's first night can be somewhat stressful for both the pup and his new family. Remember that you are setting the tone of nighttime at your house. Unless you want to play with your pup every night at 10 p.m., midnight and 2 a.m., don't initiate the habit. Your family will thank you, and soon so will your pup!

CHEMICAL TOXINS

Scour your garage for potential puppy dangers. Remove weed killers, pesticides and antifreeze materials. Antifreeze is highly toxic and just a few drops can kill a puppy or an adult dog. The sweet taste attracts the animal, who will quickly consume it from the floor or pavement.

PREVENTING PUPPY PROBLEMS

SOCIALIZATION

Now that you have done all of the preparatory work and have helped your pup get accustomed to his new home and family, it is about time for you to have some fun! Socializing your Chesapeake pup gives you the opportunity to show off your new friend, and your pup gets to reap the benefits of being an adorable furry creature that

Provide your pup with safe chew toys to satisfy his all-consuming desire to chew. Canines, especially retrievers, naturally have an oral fixation and need safe options to appease this desire.

If you intend to compete in conformation with your puppy in the future, be guided by the breeder's advice in terms of which pup shows the most promise for the show ring. Show training begins early in a pup's life!

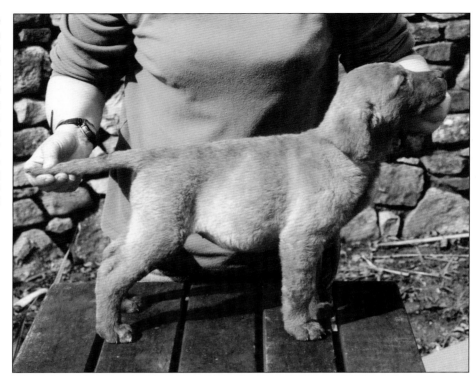

people will want to pet and, in general, think is absolutely precious!

Besides getting to know his new family, your puppy should be exposed to other people, animals and situations. This will help him become well adjusted as he grows up and less prone to being timid or fearful of the new things he

MANNERS MATTER

During the socialization process, a puppy should meet people, experience different environments and definitely be exposed to other canines. Through playing and interacting with other dogs, your puppy will learn lessons, ranging from controlling the pressure of his jaws by biting his littermates to the inner-workings of the canine pack that he will apply to his human relationships for the rest of his life. That is why removing a puppy from the litter too early (before eight weeks) can be detrimental to the pup's development.

will encounter. Of course, he must not come into close contact with dogs you don't know well until his course of injections is fully complete.

Your pup's socialization began with the breeder, but now it is your responsibility to continue it. The socialization he receives until the age of 12 weeks is the most critical, as this is the time when he forms his impressions of the outside world. Be especially careful during the eight-to-ten-week-old period, also known as the fear period. The interaction he receives during this time should be gentle and reassuring. Lack of socialization, and/or negative experiences during the socialization period, can manifest itself in fear and aggression as the dog grows up. Your puppy needs lots of positive interaction, which of course includes human contact, affection, handling and exposure to other animals.

Once your pup has received his necessary vaccinations, feel free to take him out and about (on his lead, of course). Walk him around the neighborhood, take him on your daily errands, let people pet him, let him meet other dogs and pets, etc. Puppies do not have to try to make friends; there will be no shortage of people who will want to introduce themselves. Just make sure that you carefully supervise each meeting. If the neighborhood

children want to say hello, for example, that is great—children and pups most often make great companions. However, sometimes an excited child can unintentionally handle a pup too roughly, or an overzealous pup can playfully nip a little too hard. You want to make socialization experiences positive ones. What a pup learns during this very formative stage will affect his attitude toward future encounters. You want your

IN DUE TIME
It will take at least two weeks for your puppy to become accustomed to his new surroundings. Give him lots of love, attention, handling, frequent opportunities to relieve himself, a diet he likes to eat and a place he can call his own.

PUP MEETS WORLD

Thorough socialization includes not only meeting new people but also being introduced to new experiences such as riding in the car, having his coat brushed, hearing the television, walking in a crowd—the list is endless. The more your pup experiences, and the more positive the experiences are, the less of a shock and the less frightening it will be for your pup to encounter new things.

Your Chessie has spent his first two months of life among his littermates, so being removed from this familiar environment can be unsettling for the youngster. Give him time and lots of love to feel comfortable in his new home.

dog to be comfortable around everyone. A pup that has a bad experience with a child may grow up to be a dog that is shy around or aggressive toward children.

CONSISTENCY IN TRAINING

Dogs, being pack animals, naturally need a leader, or else they try to establish dominance in their packs. When you welcome a dog into your family, the choice of who becomes the leader and who becomes the pack is entirely up to you! Your pup's intuitive quest for dominance, coupled with the fact that it is nearly impossible to look at an adorable Chesapeake pup with his "puppy-dog" eyes and not cave in, give the pup almost an unfair advantage in getting the upper hand! A pup will definitely test the waters to see what he can and cannot do. Do not give in to those pleading eyes—stand your ground when it comes to disciplining the pup and make sure that all family members do the same. It will only confuse the pup if Mother tells him to get off the sofa when he is used to sitting up there with Father to watch the nightly news. Avoid discrepancies by having all members of the household decide on the rules before the pup even comes home…and be consistent in enforcing them! Early training shapes the Chessie's personality, so you cannot be unclear in what you expect.

COMMON PUPPY PROBLEMS

The best way to prevent puppy problems is to be proactive in stopping an undesirable behavior as soon as it starts. The old saying "You can't teach an old dog new tricks" does not necessarily hold true, but it *is* true that it is much easier to discourage bad behavior in a young developing pup than to wait until the pup's bad behavior becomes the adult dog's bad habit.

Like anything else that requires love and care, a Chessie pup will grow into a beautiful companion animal that will bring joy and pride to you for years to come.

THE COCOA WARS

Chocolate contains the chemical thebromine, which is poisonous to dogs, although "chocolates" especially made for dogs are safe (as they don't actually contain chocolate) but not recommended. Any item that encourages your dog to enjoy the taste of cocoa should be discouraged. You should also exercise caution when using mulch in your garden. This frequently contains cocoa hulls, and dogs have been known to die from eating the mulch.

There are some problems that are especially prevalent in puppies as they develop.

NIPPING

As puppies start to teethe, they feel the need to sink their teeth into anything available…unfortunately, that usually includes your fingers, arms, hair and toes. You may find this behavior cute for the first five seconds…until you feel just how sharp those puppy teeth are. Nipping is something you want to discourage immediately and consistently with a firm "No!" (or whatever number of firm "Nos" it takes for him to understand that you mean business). Then, replace your finger with an appropriate chew toy. While this behavior is merely annoying when the dog is young, it can become dangerous as your Chesapeake's adult teeth grow in and his jaws develop if he is not taught that nipping is inappropriate behavior. Your Chessie does not mean any harm with a friendly nip, but he also does not know his own strength.

CRYING/WHINING

Your pup will often cry, whine, whimper, howl or make some type of commotion when he is left alone. This is basically his way of calling out for attention to make sure that you know he is there and that you have not forgotten about him. Your puppy feels insecure when he is left alone, when you are out of the house and he is in his crate or when you are in another part of the house and he cannot see you. The noise he is making is an expression of the anxiety he feels at being alone, so he needs to be taught that being alone is okay. You are not actually training the dog to stop making noise; rather, you are training him to feel comfortable when he is alone and thus removing the need for him to make the noise.

This is where the crate with cozy bedding and a toy comes in handy. You want to know that your pup is safe when you are not there to supervise, and you know that he will be safe in his crate rather than roaming freely about

These two toddlers are wrestling with one another, learning the "rules of the game." In the dog world, play is as important as work.

the house. In order for the pup to stay in his crate without making a fuss, he first needs to be comfortable in his crate. On that note, it is extremely important that the crate is never used as a form of punishment; this will cause the pup to view the crate as a negative place, rather than as a place of his own for safety and retreat.

Accustom the pup to the crate

PROPER SOCIALIZATION

The socialization period for puppies is from age 8 to 16 weeks. This is the time when puppies need to leave their birth family and take up residence with their new owners, where they will meet many new people, other pets, etc. Failure to be adequately socialized can cause the dog to grow up fearing others and being shy and unfriendly due to a lack of self-confidence.

THE PROBLEM CHILD

Training your puppy takes much patience and can be frustrating at times, but you should see results from your efforts. If you have a puppy that seems untrainable, take him to a trainer or behaviorist. The dog may have a personality problem that requires the help of a professional, or perhaps you need help in learning how to train your dog.

A beautiful bright-eyed pup, looking ahead to a wonderful future as your best friend!

in short, gradually increasing time intervals in which you put him in the crate, maybe with a treat, and stay in the room with him. If he cries or makes a fuss, do not go to him, but stay in his sight. Gradually he will realize that staying in his crate is just fine without your help, and it will not be so traumatic for him when you are not around. You may want to leave the radio on softly when you leave the house; the sound of human voices may be comforting.

CHESAPEAKE BAY RETRIEVER

DIETARY AND FEEDING CONSIDERATIONS

Today the choices of food for your Chesapeake are many and varied. There are simply dozens of brands of food in all sorts of flavors and textures, ranging from puppy diets to those for seniors. There are even hypoallergenic and low-calorie diets available. Because your Chessie's food has a bearing on coat, health and temperament, it is essential that the most suitable diet is selected for a Chesapeake of his age. It is fair to say, however, that even experienced owners can be perplexed by the enormous range of foods available. Only understanding what is best for your dog will help you reach an informed decision.

Dog foods are produced in three basic types: dry, semi-moist and canned. Dry foods are useful for the cost-conscious, for overall they tend to be less expensive than semi-moist or canned foods. Dry foods also contain the least fat and the most preservatives. In general, canned foods are made up of 60–70% water, while semi-moist ones often contain so much sugar that they are perhaps the least preferred by owners, even though their dogs seem to like them.

When selecting your dog's diet, three stages of development must be considered: the puppy

STORING DOG FOOD

You must store your dry dog food carefully. Open packages of dog food quickly lose their vitamin value, usually within 90 days of being opened. Mold spores and vermin could also contaminate the food.

Littermates compete for food, adding a little incentive at mealtime! Chessies rarely need incentive to eat, though your puppy could become finicky if you vary his diet too much.

stage, the adult stage and the senior stage.

PUPPY STAGE

Puppies instinctively want to suck milk from their dam's teats; a normal puppy will exhibit this behavior just a few moments following birth. If puppies do not attempt to suckle within the first half-hour or so, the breeder should encourage them to do so by placing them on the nipples, having selected ones with plenty of milk. This early milk supply is important in providing the essential colostrum, which protects the puppies during the first eight to ten weeks of their lives. Although a dam's milk is much better than any milk formula, despite there being some excellent ones available, if the puppies do not feed, the breeder will have to feed them by hand. For those with less experience, advice from a veterinarian is important so that not only the right quantity of milk is fed but also that of correct quality, fed at suitably frequent intervals, usually every two hours during the first few days of life.

Puppies should be allowed to nurse from their dam for about the first six weeks, although, starting around the third or fourth week, the breeder will begin to introduce small portions of suitable solid food. Most breeders like to introduce alternate milk and meat meals initially, building up to weaning time.

"DOES THIS COLLAR MAKE ME LOOK FAT?"

While humans may obsess about how they look and how trim their bodies are, many people believe that extra weight on their dogs is a good thing. The truth is, pets should not be over- or under-weight, as both can lead to or signal sickness. In order to tell how fit your pet is, run your hands over his ribs. Are his ribs buried under a layer of fat or are they sticking out considerably? If your pet is within his normal weight range, you should be able to feel the ribs easily, but they should not protrude abnormally. If you stand above him, the outline of his body should resemble an hourglass. Some breeds do tend to be leaner while some are a bit stockier, but making sure your dog is the right weight for his breed will certainly contribute to his good health.

By the time the puppies are seven or a maximum of eight weeks old, they should be fully weaned and fed solely on a proprietary puppy food. Selection of the most suitable, good-quality diet at this time is essential, for a puppy's fastest growth rate is during the first year of life. For the first year, feed a diet that is specifically designed for large, fast-growing breeds. Such foods are lower in fat and protein and are designed to prevent strain on the vulnerable, rapid-growing joints of the youngster.

Veterinarians and breeders are usually able to offer helpful advice regarding the best diet for our developing puppy. Although the frequency of meals will be reduced over time, only when a young dog has reached the age of about 12 months should an adult diet be fed. Puppy and junior diets should be well balanced for the needs of your dog so that, except in certain circumstances, additional vitamins, minerals and proteins will not be required.

ADULT DIETS

A dog is considered an adult when he has stopped growing. Although the Chessie will continue to mature physically past one year of age, in general the diet of a Chesapeake can be changed to an adult one at about one year old. Rely upon your breeder, your veterinarian or a dietary specialist to recommend

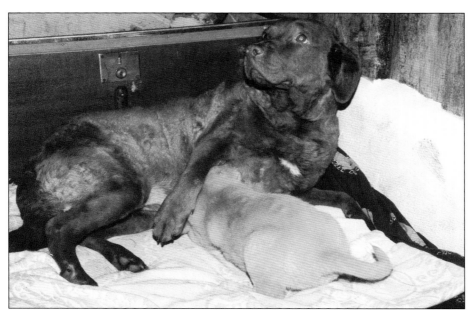

Puppies typically nurse for the first six weeks or so. This eight-week-old pup is on "last call!"

FEEDING TIPS

- Dog food must be served at room temperature, neither too hot nor too cold. Fresh water, changed often and served in a clean bowl, is mandatory, especially when feeding dry food.
- Never feed your dog from the table while you are eating, and never feed your dog leftovers from your own meal. They usually contain too much fat and too much seasoning.
- Dogs must chew their food. Hard pellets are excellent; soups and stews are to be avoided.
- Don't add leftovers or any extras to commercial dog food. The normal food is usually balanced, and adding something extra destroys the balance.
- Except for age-related changes, dogs do not require dietary variations. They can be fed the same diet, day after day, without their becoming bored or ill.

an acceptable adult-maintenance diet. Major dog-food manufacturers specialize in this type of food, and it is merely necessary for you to select the one best suited to your dog's needs. Active dogs have different requirements from more sedate dogs.

SENIOR DIETS

A switch to senior food is often determined by the activity level and role of the individual dog. Dogs who remain extremely healthy and active into their senior years (after seven to eight years of age) can continue with a maintenance or even a performance diet. Diet changes for those dogs then would be appropriate if the dog starts gaining too much weight. The average house pet who hunts occasionally could switch to a senior food at about eight years of age, the age at which most veterinarians consider dogs to be "senior."

As your dog gets older, few of his organs function up to par. The kidneys slow down and the intestines become less efficient. These age-related factors are best handled with a change in diet and a change in feeding schedule to give smaller portions that are more easily digested. There is no single best diet for every older dog. While many dogs do well on light or senior diets, other dogs do better on special premium diets such as lamb and rice. Be sen-

A Worthy Investment

Veterinary studies have proven that a balanced high-quality diet pays off in your dog's coat quality, behavior and activity level. Invest in premium brands for the maximum payoff with your dog.

sitive to your senior Chesapeake's diet, as this will help control other problems that may arise with your old friend.

WATER

Just as your dog needs proper nutrition from his food, water is an essential "nutrient" as well. Water keeps the dog's body properly hydrated and promotes normal function of the body's systems. During house-training, it is necessary to keep an eye on how much water your Chesapeake pup is drinking, but once he is reliably trained he should have access to clean fresh water at all times, especially if you feed dry food. Make certain that the dog's water bowl is clean and elevated, and change the water often.

Milk meals are introduced to pups as part of the weaning process, but milk is rarely a part of a dog's diet once fully weaned.

> ### TIPPING THE SCALES
> Good nutrition is vital to your dog's health, but many people end up over-feeding or giving unnecessary supplements. Here are some common doggie diet don'ts:
> - Adding milk, yogurt and cheese to your dog's diet may seem like a good idea for coat and skin care, but dairy products are very fattening and can cause indigestion.
> - Diets high in fat will not cause heart attacks in dogs but will certainly cause your dog to gain weight.
> - Most importantly, don't assume your dog will simply stop eating once he doesn't need any more food. Given the chance, he will eat you out of house and home!

EXERCISE FOR THE CHESSIE

Exercise is vital for all working and sporting breeds, and the Chessie requires vigorous daily exercise to stay healthy and content. This is a very active breed that welcomes outdoor physical activity and plenty of it. A puppy, however, should not be permitted to overdo it. During the first year, when the growth plates are still forming and the joints are most vulnerable, refrain from exercise that involves impact on the pup's front and rear legs. Also, to prevent bloat, exercise should be restricted for at least an hour before and after mealtimes for Chessies of all ages.

Exercising your Chesapeake can be enjoyable and healthy for both of you. Regular walks, once the puppy reaches three or four months of age, will stimulate heart rates and build muscle for both dog and owner. As the dog reaches adulthood, the speed and distance of the walks can be increased as long as they are both kept reasonable and comfortable for both of you.

Play sessions in the yard and letting the dog run free in a secure area under your supervision also are sufficient forms of exercise for the Chesapeake. Fetching games can be played indoors or out; these are excellent for giving your dog active play that he will enjoy. Chasing things that move comes naturally to retriever breeds, and

no special instructions are necessary to teach a Chessie to fetch! If you choose to play games outdoors, you must have a securely fenced-in yard and/or have the dog attached to at least an 25-foot light line for security. You want your Chesapeake to run, but not run away!

Bear in mind that an overweight dog should never be suddenly over-exercised; instead, he should be encouraged to increase exercise slowly. Also remember that not only is exercise essential to keep the dog's body fit, it is essential to his mental well-being. A bored Chessie will find something to do, which often manifests itself in some type of destructive behavior. In this sense, exercise is just as essential for the owner's mental well-being!

GROOMING YOUR CHESSIE
The Chesapeake's coat should be springy and resilient to the touch, neither soft nor smooth. It is relatively maintenance-free, and a weekly brushing with a rubber

Regular walks with your Chessie(s) will require your time each day. If you own more than one dog, you will have the advantage of the dogs' giving each other plenty of exercise by running and playing with each other. Only well-trained dogs could be walked in a trio like these Chessies!

Although a flying disk isn't nearly as much fun as retrieving as a duck, Chessies are naturally gifted at this sport and enjoy retrieving games immensely.

Your local pet shop will have a variety of grooming tools with which you can maintain your Chessie's coat in good condition.

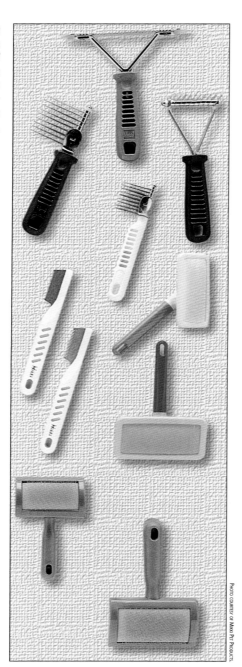

PHOTO COURTESY OF MIKKI PET PRODUCTS.

GROOMING EQUIPMENT

Invest in quality grooming equipment that will last you and your Chessie for many years to come. Here are some basics for keeping your Chessie's coat in top condition:

- Rubber brush
- Hound glove
- Rubber mat
- Dog shampoo
- Spray hose attachment
- Towels
- Ear cleaner
- Cotton balls
- Nail clippers
- Canine toothbrush
- Canine toothpaste

brush or a hound glove will keep it clean and help distribute the oils evenly throughout the coat, while removing any debris and dead hair. Do not use a wire slicker brush, rake or bristle brush for grooming, as those tools can break down the natural wave and kink in the coat. Frequent bathing is not necessary, since it can strip the coat of the natural oils necessary for a healthy coat. The Chesapeake is a double-coated breed that sheds its insulating undercoat twice a year. Twice-weekly brushing during periods of heavy shedding will help keep dead hair under control.

BATHING

Dogs do not need to be bathed as often as humans, and Chessies do not need to be bathed as often as most other dogs. Yet, occasional bathing is helpful for healthy skin and a clean, shiny coat. Since Chessies adore water, there is rarely a problem acclimating the dog to the bath.

Brush your Chesapeake thoroughly before wetting his coat. This will get rid of most mats and debris, which are harder to remove when the coat is wet. Make certain that your dog has a good non-slip surface on which to stand. Begin by wetting the dog's coat, checking the water temperature to make sure that it is neither too hot nor too cold. A shower or hose attachment is necessary for

thoroughly wetting and rinsing the coat.

Next, apply shampoo to the dog's coat and work it into a good lather. Wash the head last, as you do not want shampoo to drip into the dog's eyes while you are washing the rest of his body. You should use only a shampoo that is made for dogs. Do not use a product made for human hair. Work the shampoo all the way down to the skin. You can use this opportunity to check the skin for any bumps, bites or other abnormalities. Do not neglect any area of the body—get all of the hard-to-reach places.

Once the dog has been thoroughly shampooed, he requires an equally thorough rinsing. Shampoo left in the coat can be irritating to the dog's skin. Protect his eyes from the shampoo by shielding them with your hand

As water dogs who love to swim on a regular basis, your Chessie will not need to be bathed as often as other dogs. In fact, too-frequent bathing can ruin the natural properties of his coat that repel dirt and water.

BATHING BEAUTY

Once you are sure that the dog is thoroughly rinsed, squeeze the excess water out of his coat with your hand and dry him with a heavy towel. You may choose to use a blow dryer on his coat or just let it dry naturally. In cold weather, never allow your dog outside with a wet coat.

There are "dry bath" products on the market, which are sprays and powders intended for spot cleaning, that can be used between regular baths if necessary. They are not substitutes for regular baths, but they are easy to use for touch-ups as they do not require rinsing.

Start brushing the puppy when he is young so that he learns to accept the routine. A soft brush is a good tool for the puppy coat.

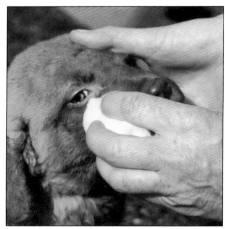

Tear stains or dirt around the eyes can be removed with a soft cotton wipe. Pet shops often carry cleansing solution to assist in the process.

As part of your regular grooming routine, inspect your Chessie's ears. Only clean the part of the ear that you can see. *Never* probe into the canal.

and directing the flow of water in the opposite direction. You should also avoid getting water in the ear canal. Be prepared for your dog to shake out his coat—you might want to stand back, but make sure you have a hold on him to keep him from running through the house. Have a heavy towel close at hand.

EAR CLEANING

The ears should be kept clean with a cotton ball and ear powder or liquid made especially for dogs. Do not probe into the ear canal with a cotton swab, as this

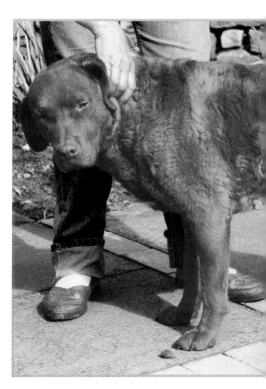

can cause injury. Be on the lookout for any signs of infection or ear-mite infestation. If your Chesapeake has been shaking his head or scratching at his ears frequently, this usually indicates a problem. If the dog's ears have an unusual odor, this is a sure sign of mite infestation or infection, and a signal to have his ears checked by the veterinarian.

NAIL CLIPPING

Your Chesapeake should be accustomed to having his nails trimmed at an early age since nail clipping will be part of your

In light-colored nails, like those on this Chessie pup, it is easy to see the quick.

Nails that are dark in color make the quick undetectable. Clip only a little at a time with black-nailed dogs.

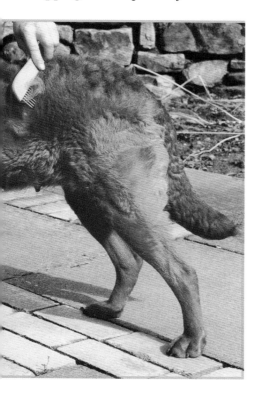

maintenance routine throughout his life. Not only does it look nicer, but long nails can scratch someone unintentionally. Also, a long nail has a better chance of ripping and bleeding, or of causing the feet to spread. A good rule of thumb is that if you can hear your dog's nails' clicking on the floor when he walks, his nails are too long.

Before you start cutting, make sure you can identify the "quick" in each nail. The quick is a blood vessel that runs through the center of each nail and grows rather close to the end. The quick will bleed if accidentally cut, which

The double-coated Chessie sheds his undercoat twice a year. Combing and brushing removes the dead hair from the dog during these shedding periods.

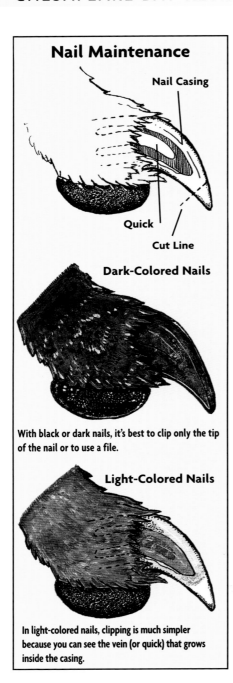

Nail Maintenance

Nail Casing

Quick

Cut Line

Dark-Colored Nails

With black or dark nails, it's best to clip only the tip of the nail or to use a file.

Light-Colored Nails

In light-colored nails, clipping is much simpler because you can see the vein (or quick) that grows inside the casing.

will be quite painful for the dog as it contains nerve endings. Keep some type of clotting agent on hand, such as a styptic pencil or styptic powder (the type used for shaving). This will stop the bleeding quickly when applied to the end of the cut nail. Do not panic if you cut the quick, just stop the bleeding and talk soothingly to your dog. Once he has calmed down, move on to the next nail. It is better to clip a little at a time, particularly with black-nailed dogs.

Hold your pup steady as you begin trimming his nails; you do not want him to make any sudden movements or run away. Talk to him soothingly and stroke him as you clip. Holding his foot in your hand, simply take off the end of each nail with one swift clip. You should purchase nail clippers that are made for use on dogs; you can probably find them wherever you buy pet supplies.

TRAVELING WITH YOUR DOG

CAR TRAVEL

You should accustom your Chesapeake to riding in a car at an early age. You may or may not take him in the car often, but at the very least he will need to go to the vet and you do not want these trips to be traumatic for the dog or troublesome for you. The safest way for a dog to ride in the car is in his crate. If he uses a crate in

DEADLY DECAY

Did you know that periodontal disease (a condition of the bone and gums surrounding a tooth) can be fatal? Having your dog's teeth and mouth checked yearly, as well as making home dental-care part of your grooming routine, can prevent it.

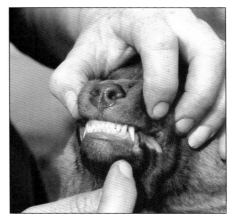

Home dental-care should begin when your Chessie is a puppy. Report any irregularities, such as retained puppy teeth, to your vet.

the house, you can use the same crate for travel.

Put the pup in the crate and see how he reacts. If he seems uneasy, you can have a passenger hold him on his lap while you drive. Other options for car travel include a specially made safety harness for dogs, which straps the dog in much like a seat belt, or a partition for the back part of the vehicle (for sport-utility or similar larger vehicles) to create a safe area for the dog. Regardless of which option you choose, never let the dog roam loose in the vehicle—this is very dangerous! If you should stop short, your dog can be thrown and injured. If the dog starts climbing on you and pestering you while you are driving, you will not be able to concentrate on the road. It is an unsafe situation for everyone—human and canine.

For long trips, be prepared to stop to let the dog relieve himself. Take with you whatever you need to clean up after him, including some paper towels and perhaps

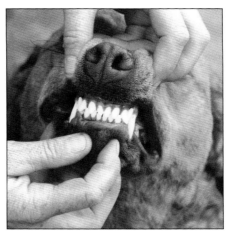

The adult's teeth should be strong and white and meet in a scissor bite.

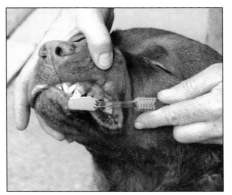

Yes, you should brush your Chessie's teeth, though not as often as you do your own. Once a week should suffice for the dog's teeth.

some old rags for use should he have a potty accident in the car or suffer from motion sickness.

AIR TRAVEL

Contact your chosen airline before proceeding with travel plans that include your Chessie. The dog will be required to travel in a fiberglass crate and you should always check in advance with the airline regarding specific requirements for the crate's size, type and labeling, as well as any travel restrictions or necessary health certificates.

To help put the dog at ease for the flight, give him one of his favorite toys in the crate. Do not feed your Chessie for several hours prior to checking in so that you minimize his need to relieve himself. Some airlines require you to provide documentation as to when the dog was last fed. In any case, a light meal is best. For long trips, you will have to attach food and water bowls to the outside of your dog's crate so that airline

employees can tend to him between legs of the trip.

Make sure that your dog is properly identified and that your contact information appears on his ID tags and on his crate. Your Chessie will travel in a different area of the plane than the human passengers, so every rule must be strictly followed to prevent any risk of getting separated from your dog.

VACATIONS AND BOARDING

So you want to take a family vacation—and you want to include *all* members of the family. You would probably make arrangements for accommodations ahead of time anyway, but this is especially important when traveling with a dog. You do not want to make an overnight stop at the only place around for miles, only to find out that dogs are not allowed. Also, you do not want to reserve a place for your family without confirming that you are traveling with a dog, because, if it is against the hotel's policy, you may end up without a place to stay.

Alternatively, if you are traveling and choose not to bring your Chesapeake, you will have to make arrangements for him while you are away. Some options are to take him to a friend's house to stay while you are gone, to have a trusted neighbor stop by often or stay at your house or to take your

---

TRAVEL TIP

Never leave your dog alone in the car. In hot weather, your dog can die from the high temperature inside a closed vehicle; even a car parked in the shade can heat up very quickly. Leaving the window open is dangerous as well since the dog can hurt himself trying to get out.

TRAVELING ABROAD

For international travel, you will have to make arrangements well in advance (perhaps months), as countries' regulations pertaining to bringing in animals differ. There may be special health certificates and/or vaccinations that your dog will need before taking the trip; sometimes this has to be done within a certain time frame. When traveling to rabies-free countries, you will need to bring proof of the dog's rabies vaccination and there may be a quarantine period upon arrival.

dog to a reputable boarding kennel. If you choose to board him at a kennel, you should visit in advance to see the facilities provided and where the dogs are kept. Are the dogs' areas spacious and kept clean? Talk to some of the employees and see how they treat the dogs—do they spend time with the dogs, play with them, exercise them, etc.? Also find out the kennel's policy on vaccinations and what they require. This is for all of the dogs' safety, since there is a greater risk of diseases being passed from dog to dog when dogs are kept together.

IDENTIFICATION

Your Chesapeake is your valued companion and friend. That is why you always keep a close eye on him and you have made sure that he cannot escape from the yard or wriggle out of his collar and run away from you. However, accidents can happen and there may come a time when your dog unexpectedly becomes separated from you. If this unfortunate event should occur, the first thing on your mind will be finding him. Proper identification, including an ID tag and possibly a tattoo and/or microchip, will increase the chances of his being returned to you safely and quickly.

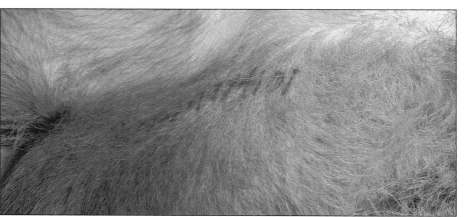

Tattooing is a desirable form of identification as it is more permanent than an ID tag. However, a tattoo is not a substitute for the ID tag attached to the dog's collar, which gives the owner's contact information.

CHESAPEAKE BAY RETRIEVER

Although the Chesapeake is frequently compared to the Labrador Retriever, the Chessie is more challenging—and rewarding—than that most popular of retrievers. Chessies have minds of their own and require more persistence to overcome their stubborn, mindful ways. Chessies march to the beat of their own drummer!

Living with an untrained dog is a lot like owning a piano that you do not know how to play—it is a nice object to look at, but it does not do much more than that to bring you pleasure. Now try taking piano lessons, and suddenly the piano comes alive and brings forth magical sounds and rhythms that set your heart singing and your body swaying. The same is true with your Chesapeake. Any dog is a big responsibility and, if not trained sensibly, may develop unacceptable behavior that annoys you or could even cause family friction.

To train your Chessie, you may like to enroll in an obedience class. Teach your dog good manners as you learn how and why he behaves the way he does. Find out how to communicate with your dog and how to recognize and understand his communications with you. Suddenly the dog takes on a new role in your life—he is clever, interesting, well behaved and fun to be with. He demonstrates his bond of devotion to you daily. In other words, your Chesapeake does wonders for your ego because he constantly reminds you that you are not only his leader, you are his hero!

Your Chessie pup looks up to you for care and guidance, and puppyhood is the time to instill the house rules and good behavior.

Those involved with teaching dog obedience and counseling owners about their dogs' behavior have discovered some interesting facts about dog ownership. For example, training dogs when they are puppies results in the highest rate of success in developing well-mannered and well-adjusted adult dogs. Training an older dog, from six months to six years of age, can produce almost equal results, providing that the owner accepts the dog's slower rate of learning capability and is willing to work patiently to help the dog succeed at developing to his fullest potential. Unfortunately, many owners of untrained adult dogs lack the patience factor, so they do not persist until their dogs are successful at learning particular behaviors.

Training a puppy aged 10 to 16 weeks (20 weeks at the most) is like working with a dry sponge in a pool of water. The pup soaks up whatever you show him and constantly looks for more things to do and learn. At this early age, his body is not yet producing hormones, and therein lies the reason for such a high rate of success. Without hormones, he is focused on his owners and not particularly interested in investigating other places, dogs, people, etc. You are his leader: his provider of food, water, shelter and security. He latches onto you

REAP THE REWARDS

If you start with a normal, healthy dog and give him time, patience and some carefully executed lessons, you will reap the rewards of that training for the life of the dog. And what a life it will be! The two of you will find immeasurable pleasure in the companionship you have built together with love, respect and understanding.

and wants to stay close. He will usually follow you from room to room, will not let you out of his sight when you are outdoors with him and will respond in like manner to the people and animals you encounter. If you greet a friend warmly, he will be happy to greet the person as well. If, however, you are hesitant about the approach of a stranger, he will respond accordingly.

> **PARENTAL GUIDANCE**
> Training a dog is a life experience. Many parents admit that much of what they know about raising children they learned from caring for their dogs. Dogs respond to love, fairness and guidance, just as children do. Become a good dog owner and you may become an even better parent.

Incorporate some fun into your training sessions to keep your Chessie motivated and interested. Any Chessie will welcome a chance to fetch!

Once the puppy begins to produce hormones, his natural curiosity emerges and he begins to investigate the world around him. It is at this time when you may notice that the untrained dog begins to wander away from you and even ignore your commands to stay close. When this behavior becomes a problem, you have two choices: get rid of the dog or train him. It is strongly urged that you choose the latter option.

You usually will be able to find obedience classes within a reasonable distance from your home, but you can also do a lot to train your dog yourself. Sometimes there are classes available, but the tuition is too costly. Whatever the circumstances, the solution to training your Chessie without obedience classes lies within the pages of this book.

This chapter is devoted to helping you train your Chesapeake at home. If the recommended procedures are followed faithfully, you may expect

CANINE DEVELOPMENT SCHEDULE

It is important to understand how and at what age a puppy develops into adulthood. If you are a puppy owner, consult the following Canine Development Schedule to determine the stage of development your puppy is currently experiencing. This knowledge will help you as you work with the puppy in the weeks and months ahead.

Period	Age	Characteristics
FIRST TO THIRD	BIRTH TO SEVEN WEEKS	Puppy needs food, sleep and warmth, and responds to simple and gentle touching. Needs mother for security and disciplining. Needs littermates for learning and interacting with other dogs. Pup learns to function within a pack and learns pack order of dominance. Begin socializing pup with adults and children for short periods. Pup begins to become aware of his environment.
FOURTH	EIGHT TO TWELVE WEEKS	Brain is fully developed. Pup needs socializing with outside world. Remove from mother and littermates. Needs to change from canine pack to human pack. Human dominance necessary. Fear period occurs between 8 and 12 weeks. Avoid fright and pain.
FIFTH	THIRTEEN TO SIXTEEN WEEKS	Training and formal obedience should begin. Less association with other dogs, more with people, places, situations. Period will pass easily if you remember this is pup's change-to-adolescence time. Be firm and fair. Flight instinct prominent. Permissiveness and over-disciplining can do permanent damage. Praise for good behavior.
JUVENILE	FOUR TO EIGHT MONTHS	Another fear period about 7 to 8 months of age. It passes quickly, but be cautious of fright and pain. Sexual maturity reached. Dominant traits established. Dog should understand sit, down, come and stay by now.

NOTE: THESE ARE APPROXIMATE TIME FRAMES. ALLOW FOR INDIVIDUAL DIFFERENCES IN PUPPIES.

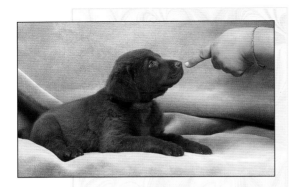

THINK BEFORE YOU BARK
Dogs are sensitive to their masters' moods and emotions. Use your voice wisely when communicating with your dog. Never raise your voice at your dog unless you are trying to correct him. "Barking" at your dog can become as meaningless as "dogspeak" is to you.

Breeders who acclimate young pups to crates are doing future owners a great favor. Teaching a pup to feel comfortable and content in a crate is half the battle of training him to proper toileting.

positive results that will prove rewarding to both you and your dog.

Whether your new charge is a puppy or a mature adult, the methods of teaching and the techniques we use in training basic behaviors are the same. After all, no dog, whether puppy or adult, likes harsh or inhumane methods. All creatures, however, respond favorably to gentle motivational methods and sincere praise and encourage-ment. Now let us get started.

HOUSEBREAKING
You can train a puppy to relieve himself wherever you choose, but

this must be somewhere suitable. You should bear in mind from the outset that when your puppy is old enough to go out in public places, any canine deposits must be removed at once. You will always have to carry with you a small plastic bag or "poop-scoop."

Outdoor training includes such surfaces as grass, soil and cement. Indoor training usually means training your dog to newspaper (not the best option with a large dog like the Chessie!). When deciding on the surface and location that you will want your Chesapeake to use, be

The ideal relief site should be a grassy part of your yard in an out-of-the-way area.

sure it is going to be permanent. Training your dog to grass and then changing your mind a few months later is extremely difficult for both dog and owner.

Next, choose the command you will use each and every time you want your puppy to void. "Hurry up" and "Let's go" are examples of commands commonly used by dog owners. Get in the habit of giving the puppy your chosen relief command before you take him out. That way, when he becomes an adult, you will be able to determine if he wants to go out when you ask him. A confirmation will be signs of interest, such as wagging his tail, watching you intently, going to the door, etc.

SAFETY FIRST

While it may seem that the most important things to your dog are eating, sleeping and chewing the upholstery on your furniture, his first concern is actually safety. The domesticated dogs we keep as companions have the same pack instinct as their ancestors who ran free thousands of years ago. Because of this pack instinct, your dog wants to know that he and his pack are not in danger of being harmed, and that his pack has a strong, capable leader. You must establish yourself as the leader early on in your relationship. That way your dog will trust that you will take care of him and the pack, and he will accept your commands without question.

Once the male discovers the joy of a tree in his yard, he will use it regularly to relieve himself.

PUPPY'S NEEDS

The puppy needs to relieve himself after play periods, after each meal, after he has been sleeping and at any time he indicates that he is looking for a place to urinate or defecate. The urinary and intestinal tract muscles of very young puppies are not fully developed. Therefore, like human babies, puppies need to relieve themselves frequently.

Take your puppy out often—every hour for an eight-week-old, for example—and always immediately after sleeping and eating. The older the puppy, the less often he will need to relieve himself. Finally, as a mature healthy adult, he will require only three to five relief trips per day.

HOUSING

Since the types of housing and control you provide for your puppy have a direct relationship on the success of house-training, we consider the various aspects of both before we begin training.

Taking a new puppy home and turning him loose in your house can be compared to turning a child loose in an amusement park and telling the child that the place is all his! The sheer enormity of the place would be too much for him to handle. Instead, offer the puppy clearly defined areas where he can play, sleep, eat and live. A room of the house where the family gathers is the most obvious choice. Puppies are social animals and need to feel a part of the pack right from the start. Hearing your voice, watching you while you are doing things and smelling you nearby are all positive reinforcers that he is now a member of your

CALM DOWN
Dogs will do anything for your attention. If you reward the dog when he is calm and attentive, you will develop a well-mannered dog. If, on the other hand, you greet your dog excitedly and encourage him to wrestle with you, the dog will greet you the same way and you will have a hyperactive dog on your hands.

pack. Usually a family room, the kitchen or a nearby adjoining breakfast area is ideal for providing safety and security for both puppy and owner.

Within the designated room, there should be a smaller area that the puppy can call his own. An alcove, a wire or fiberglass dog crate or a partitioned (not boarded!) corner from which he can view the activities of his new family will be fine. The size of the area or crate is the key factor here. The area must be large enough so that the puppy can lie down and stretch out, as well as stand up, without rubbing his head on the top. At the same time, it must be small enough so that he cannot relieve himself at one end and sleep at the other without coming into contact with his droppings. Dogs are, by nature, clean animals and will not remain close to their relief areas unless forced to do so. In those cases, they then become dirty dogs and usually remain that way for life.

The dog's designated area should contain clean bedding and a toy. Water should be available in a non-spill container, although, during housebreaking, you'll want to be aware of when your pup is drinking so you'll now when he needs "to go."

CONTROL

By *control*, we mean helping the puppy to create a lifestyle pattern

THE CLEAN LIFE
By providing sleeping and resting quarters that fit the dog, and offering frequent opportunities to relieve himself outside his quarters, the puppy quickly learns that the outdoors is the place to go when he needs to urinate or defecate. It also reinforces his innate desire to keep his sleeping quarters clean. This, in turn, helps develop the muscle control that will eventually produce a reliably house-trained dog with clean living habits.

The effort you put into crate-training your puppy will result in an adult Chessie who welcomes time in his very own den.

HOUSE-TRAINING TIP

Most of all, be consistent. Always take your dog to the same location, always use the same command and always have the dog on lead when he is in his relief area, unless a fenced-in yard is available.

By following the method described in this chapter, your puppy will be completely house-trained by the time his muscle and brain development reach maturity. While small breeds usually mature faster than large breeds, all puppies should be trained by six months of age. Keep in mind, though, that males of all breeds, regardless of size or the individual breed's trainability, tend to take longer to housebreak than females.

that will be compatible to that of his human pack *(you!)*. Just as we guide little children to learn our way of life, we must show the puppy when it is time to play, eat, sleep, exercise and even entertain himself.

Your puppy should always sleep in his crate. He should also learn that, during times of household confusion and excessive human activity, such as at breakfast when family members are preparing for the day, he can play by himself in relative safety and comfort in his designated area. Each time you leave the puppy alone, he should understand exactly where he is to stay.

Puppies are chewers. They cannot tell the difference between lamp cords, television wires, shoes, table legs, etc. Chewing into an electrical wire, for example, can be fatal to the puppy, while a shorted wire can start a fire in the house. In another scenario, if the puppy chews on the arm of the chair when he is alone, you will probably discipline him angrily when you get home. Thus, he makes the association that your coming home means he is going to be punished. (He will not remember chewing the chair and is incapable of making the association of the discipline with his naughty deed.) Accustoming the pup to his designated area not only keeps him safe but also avoids his engaging in dangerous and/or destructive behaviors when you are not around.

Times of excitement, such as special occasions, family parties, etc., can be fun for the puppy, providing that he can view the activities from the security of his designated area. He is not underfoot and he is not being fed all sorts of tidbits that will probably cause him stomach distress, yet he still feels a part of the fun.

ESTABLISHING A SCHEDULE

A puppy should be taken to his relief area each time he is released from his designated area, after meals, after play sessions and when he first awakens in the morning (at age eight weeks, this can mean 5 a.m.!). The puppy will indicate that he's ready "to go" by circling or sniffing busily—do not misinterpret these signs. For a puppy less than ten weeks of age, a routine of taking him out every hour is necessary. As the puppy grows, he will be able to wait for longer periods of time.

Keep trips to his relief area short. Stay no more than five or six minutes and then return to the house. If he goes during that time, praise him lavishly and take him indoors immediately. If he does not, but he has an accident when you go back indoors, pick him up immediately, say "No! No!" and return to his relief area. Wait a few minutes, then return to the house again. Never hit a puppy or put his face in urine or excrement when he has had an accident!

Once indoors, put the puppy in his crate until you have had time to clean up his accident. Then, release him to the family area and watch him more closely than before. Chances are, his accident was a result of your not picking up his signal or waiting too long before offering him the opportunity to relieve himself. Never hold a grudge against the puppy for accidents.

Let the puppy learn that going outdoors means it is time

COMMAND STANCE
Stand up straight and authoritatively when giving your dog commands. Do not issue commands when lying on the floor or lying on your back on the sofa. If you are on your hands and knees when you give a command, your dog will think you are positioning yourself to play.

to relieve himself, not to play. Once trained, he will be able to play indoors and out and still differentiate between the times for play versus the times for relief.

Help the puppy develop regular hours for naps, being alone, playing by himself and just resting, all in his crate. Encourage him to entertain himself while you are busy with your activities. Let him learn that having you near is comforting, but it is not your main purpose in life to provide him with undivided attention.

Each time you put your

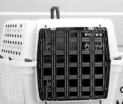

THE SUCCESS METHOD

Success that comes by luck is usually short-lived. Success that comes by well-thought-out proven methods is often more easily achieved and permanent. This is the Success Method. It is designed to give you, the puppy owner, a simple yet proven way to help your puppy develop clean living habits and a feeling of security in his new environment.

6 Steps to Successful Crate Training

1 Tell the puppy "Crate time!" and place him in the crate with a small treat (a piece of cheese or half of a biscuit). Let him stay in the crate for five minutes while you are in the same room. Then release him and praise lavishly. Never release him when he is fussing. Wait until he is quiet before you let him out.

2 Repeat Step 1 several times a day.

3 The next day, place the puppy in the crate as before. Let him stay there for ten minutes. Do this several times.

4 Continue building time in five-minute increments until the puppy stays in his crate for 30 minutes with you in the room. Always take him to his relief area after prolonged periods in his crate.

5 Now go back to Step 1 and let the puppy stay in his crate for five minutes, this time while you are out of the room.

6 Once again, build crate time in five-minute increments with you out of the room. When the puppy will stay willingly in his crate (he may even fall asleep!) for 30 minutes with you out of the room, he will be ready to stay in it for several hours at a time.

puppy in his own area, use the same command, whatever suits best. Soon he will run to his crate or special area when he hears you say those words.

Crate training provides safety for you, the puppy and the home. It also provides the puppy with a feeling of security, and that helps the puppy achieve self-confidence and clean habits. Remember that one of the primary ingredients in house-training your puppy is control. Regardless of your lifestyle, there will always be occasions when you will need to have a place where your dog can stay and be happy and safe. Crate training is the answer for now and in the future.

In conclusion, a few key elements are really all you need for a successful house-training method—consistency, frequency, praise, control and supervision.

Always clean up after your dog, whether you're in a public place or your own yard.

By following these procedures with a normal, healthy puppy, you and the puppy will soon be past the stage of accidents and ready to move on to a clean and rewarding life together.

ROLES OF DISCIPLINE, REWARD AND PUNISHMENT

Discipline, training one to act in accordance with rules, brings order to life. It is as simple as that. Without discipline, particularly in a group society, chaos will reign supreme and the group will eventually perish. Humans and canines are social animals and need some form of discipline in order to function effectively. They must procure food, reproduce to keep their species going and protect their home base and their young. If there were no discipline in the lives of social animals, they would eventually die from starvation and/or predation by other stronger animals.

In the case of domestic canines, discipline in their lives is needed in order for them to

HOW MANY TIMES A DAY?

AGE	RELIEF TRIPS
To 14 weeks	10
14–22 weeks	8
22–32 weeks	6
Adulthood	4
(dog stops growing)	

These are estimates, of course, but they are a guide to the *minimum* number of opportunities a dog should have each day to relieve himself.

results in a pleasant event tends to be repeated, and a behavior that results in an unpleasant event tends not to be repeated. It is this theory upon which training methods are based today. For example, if you manipulate a dog to perform a specific behavior and reward him for doing it, he is likely to do it again because he enjoyed the end result.

Occasionally, punishment, a penalty inflicted for an offense, is necessary. The best type of punishment often comes from an outside source. For example, a child is told not to touch the stove because he may get burned. He disobeys and touches the stove. In doing so, he receives a burn. From that time on, he respects the heat of the stove and avoids contact with it. Therefore,

How much freedom you allow your Chessie is up to you. If you allow your dog on the furniture as a pup, you can be sure that your adult dog will take up his share of the bed!

understand how their pack (you and other family members) functions and how they must act in order to survive.

A large humane society in a highly populated area recently surveyed dog owners regarding their satisfaction with their relationships with their dogs. People who had trained their dogs were 75% more satisfied with their pets than those who had never trained their dogs.

Dr. Edward Thorndike, a noted psychologist, established *Thorndike's Theory of Learning*, which states that a behavior that

LANGUAGE BARRIER

Dogs do not understand our language and have to rely on tone of voice more than just words or sound. They can be trained to react to a certain sound, at a certain volume. If you say "No, Oliver" in a very soft, pleasant voice, it will not have the same meaning as "No, Oliver!!" when you raise your voice.

You should never use the dog's name during a reprimand, just the command "No! " You never want the dog to associate his name with a negative experience or reprimand.

a behavior that results in an unpleasant event tends not to be repeated.

A good example of a dog learning the hard way is the dog who chases the house cat. He is told many times to leave the cat alone, yet he persists in teasing the cat. Then, one day, the dog begins chasing the cat but the cat turns and swipes a claw across the dog's face, leaving the dog with a painful gash on his nose. The final result is that the dog stops chasing the cat.

TRAINING EQUIPMENT

COLLAR AND LEAD
For a Chessie, the collar and lead that you use for training must be one with which you are easily able to work, not too heavy for the dog and perfectly safe.

TREATS
Have a bag of treats on hand; something nutritious and easy to swallow works best. Use a soft treat, a chunk of cheese or a piece of cooked chicken rather than a dry biscuit. By the time the dog has finished chewing a dry treat, he will forget why he is being rewarded in the first place! Using food rewards in training will not teach a dog to beg at the table—the only way to teach a dog to beg at the table is to give him food from the table. In training, rewarding the dog with a food treat will help him associate praise and the treats with learning new behaviors that obviously please his owner.

TRAINING BEGINS: ASK THE DOG A QUESTION
In order to teach your dog anything, you must first get his attention. After all, he cannot learn anything if he is looking away from you with his mind on something else.

PLAN TO PLAY
The puppy should have regular play and exercise sessions when he is with you or a family member. Exercise for a very young puppy can consist of a short walk around the house or yard. Playing can include fetching games with a large ball or a special toy. (All puppies teethe and need soft things upon which to chew.) Remember to restrict indoor play periods to his living area (the family room, for example) until he is completely house-trained.

To get your dog's attention, ask him "School?" and immediately walk over to him and give him a treat as you tell him "Good dog." Wait a minute or two and repeat the routine, this time with a treat in your hand as you approach within a foot of the dog. Do not go directly to him, but stop about a foot short of him and hold out the treat as you ask "School?" He will see you approaching with a treat in your hand and most likely begin walking toward you. As you meet, give him the treat and praise again.

The third time, ask the question, have a treat in your hand and walk only a short distance toward the dog so that he must walk almost all the way to you. As he reaches you, give him the treat and praise again.

By this time, the dog will probably be getting the idea that if he pays attention to you, especially when you ask that

> **THE GOLDEN RULE**
> The golden rule of dog training is simple. For each "question" (command), there is only one correct answer (reaction). One command = one reaction. Keep practicing the command until the dog reacts correctly without hesitating. Be repetitive but not monotonous. Dogs get bored just as people do!

question, it will pay off in treats and enjoyable activities for him. In other words, he learns that "school" means doing great things with you that are fun and that result in positive attention for him.

Remember that the dog does not understand your verbal language; he only recognizes sounds. Your question translates to a series of sounds for him, and those sounds become the signal to go to you and pay attention. The dog learns that if he does this, he will get to interact with you plus receive treats and praise.

THE BASIC COMMANDS

TEACHING SIT

Now that you have the dog's attention, attach his lead and hold it in your left hand, and hold a food treat in your right hand. Place your food hand at the dog's nose and let him lick

Engage the puppy with a treat or a toy to get his attention for a lesson. Always make the lesson fun and your pup will look forward to his training sessions with you.

the treat but not take it from you. Say "Sit" and slowly raise your food hand from in front of the dog's nose up over his head so that he is looking at the ceiling. As he bends his head upward, he will have to bend his knees to maintain his balance. As he bends his knees, he will assume a sit position. At that point, release the food treat and praise lavishly with comments such as "Good dog! Good sit!," etc. Remember to always praise enthusiastically, because dogs relish verbal praise from their owners and feel so proud of themselves whenever they accomplish a behavior.

Incidentally, you will not use food forever in getting the dog to obey your commands. Food is

PRACTICE MAKES PERFECT!

- Have training lessons with your dog every day in several short segments—three to five times a day for a few minutes at a time is ideal.
- Do not have long practice sessions. The dog will become easily bored.
- Never practice when you are tired, ill, worried or in an otherwise negative mood. This will transmit to the dog and may have an adverse effect on his performance.

Think fun, short and above all *positive!* End each session on a high note, rather than a failed exercise, and make sure to give a lot of praise. Enjoy the training and help your dog enjoy it, too.

only used to teach new behaviors and, once the dog knows what you want when you give a specific command, you will wean him off the food treats but still maintain the verbal praise. After all, you will always have your voice with you, and there will be many times when you have no food rewards but expect the dog to obey.

TEACHING DOWN

Teaching the down exercise is easy when you understand how the dog perceives the down position, and it is very difficult when you do not. Dogs perceive the down position as a submis-

The sit command is the simplest lesson and the one with which most trainers begin the dog's education. Practice this command every day, and always end a lesson on a command that the pup has mastered.

DOUBLE JEOPARDY

A dog in jeopardy never lies down. He stays alert on his feet because instinct tells him that he may have to run away or fight for his survival. Therefore, if a dog feels threatened or anxious, he will not lie down. Consequently, it is important to keep the dog calm and relaxed as he learns the down exercise.

sive one; therefore, teaching the down exercise by using a forceful method can sometimes make the dog develop such a fear of the down that he either runs away when you say "Down" or he attempts to snap at the person who tries to force him down.

Have the dog sit close alongside your left leg, facing in the same direction as you are. Hold the lead in your left hand and a food treat in your right. Now place your left hand lightly on the top of the dog's shoulders where they meet above the spinal cord. Do not push down on the dog's shoulders; simply rest your left hand there so you can guide the dog to lie down close to your left leg rather than to swing away from your side when he drops.

Now place the food hand at the dog's nose, say "Down" very softly (almost a whisper) and slowly lower the food hand to the dog's front feet. When the food hand reaches the floor, begin moving it forward along the floor in front of the dog. Keep talking softly to the dog, saying things like, "Do you want this treat? You can do this, good dog." Your reassuring tone of voice will help calm the dog as he tries to follow the food hand in order to get the treat.

When the dog's elbows touch the floor, release the food and praise softly. Try to get the dog to maintain that down position for several seconds before you let him sit up again. The goal here is to get the dog to settle down and not feel threatened in the down position.

TEACHING STAY

It is easy to teach the dog to stay in either a sit or a down position. Again, we use food and praise during the teaching process as we help the dog to understand exactly what it is that we are expecting him to do.

To teach the sit/stay, start with the dog sitting on your left side as before and hold the lead in your left hand. Have a food treat in your right hand and place your food hand at the dog's nose. Say "Stay" and step out on your right foot to stand directly in front of the dog, toe to toe, as he licks and nibbles the treat. Be sure to keep his head facing upward to maintain the sit position. Count to five and then swing around to stand next to the dog again with him on your left. As soon as you get back to the original position, release the food and praise lavishly.

To teach the down/stay, do the down as previously described. As soon as the dog lies down, say "Stay" and step out on your right foot just as you did in the sit/stay. Count to five and then return to stand beside the dog with him on your left side. Release the treat and praise as always.

Within a week or ten days, you can begin to add a bit of distance between you and your dog when you leave him. When you do, use your left hand open with the palm facing the dog as a stay signal, much the same as the hand signal a police officer uses to stop traffic at an intersection. Hold the food treat in your right hand as before, but this time the food will not be touching the dog's nose. He will watch the food hand and quickly learn that he is going to get that treat as soon as you return to his side.

When you can stand 3 feet away from your dog for 30 seconds, you can then begin building time and distance in both stays. Eventually, the dog can be expected to remain in the stay position for prolonged

Once the Chessie has learned the down command, the down-stay exercise is a natural extension that can be accomplished with practice.

disobeys outright or runs in the opposite direction. The secret, therefore, is to teach the dog a game and, when you want him to come to you, simply play the game. It is practically a no-fail solution!

To begin, have several members of your family take a few food treats and each go into a different room in the house. Everyone takes turns calling the dog, and each person should celebrate the dog's finding him with a treat and lots of happy praise. When a person calls the dog, he is actually inviting the dog to find him and to get a treat as a reward for "winning."

A few turns of the "Where are you?" game and the dog will understand that everyone is playing the game and that each person has a big celebration awaiting the dog's success at locating him or her. Once the dog learns to love the game, simply calling out "Where are you?" will bring him running from wherever

periods of time until you return to him or call him to you. Always praise lavishly when he stays.

TEACHING COME

If you make teaching "come" an exciting experience, you should never have a student that does not love the game or that fails to come when called. The secret, it seems, is never to teach the word "come."

At times when an owner most wants his dog to come when called, the owner is likely to be upset or anxious and he allows these feelings to come through in the tone of his voice when he calls his dog. Hearing that desperation in his owner's voice, the dog fears the results of going to him and therefore either

---

"COME" . . . BACK
Never call your dog to come to you for a correction or scold him when he reaches you. That is the quickest way to turn a come command into "Go away fast!" Dogs think only in the present tense, and your dog will connect the scolding with coming to you, not with the misbehavior of a few moments earlier.

he is when he hears that all-important question.

The come command is recognized as one of the most important things to teach a dog, but there are trainers who work with thousands of dogs and never teach the actual word "come." Yet these dogs will race to respond to a person who uses the dog's name followed by "Where are you?" For example, a woman has a 12-year-old companion dog who went blind, but who never fails to locate her owner when asked, "Where are you?"

Children, in particular, love to play this game with their dogs. Children can hide in smaller places like a shower or bathtub, behind a bed or under a table. The dog needs to work a little bit harder to find these hiding places, but, when he does, he loves to celebrate with a treat and a tussle with a favorite youngster.

TEACHING HEEL

Heeling means that the dog walks beside the owner without pulling. It takes time and patience on the owner's part to succeed at teaching the dog that he (the owner) will not proceed unless the dog is walking calmly beside him. Neither pulling out ahead on the lead nor lagging behind is acceptable.

Begin by holding the lead in your left hand as the dog sits beside your left leg. Move the loop end of the lead to your right hand, but keep your left hand short on the lead so that it keeps the dog in close next to you.

Say "Heel" and step forward on your left foot. Keep the dog close to you and take three steps. Stop and have the dog sit next to you in what we now call the heel position. Praise verbally, but do not touch the dog. Hesitate a moment and begin again with "Heel," taking three steps and stopping, at which point the dog is told to sit again.

Your goal here is to have the

HEELING WELL

Teach your dog to heel in an enclosed area. Once you think the dog will obey reliably and you want to attempt advanced obedience exercises such as off-lead heeling, test him in a fenced-in area so he cannot run away.

Never overlook the "retriever" in your Chessie's name when it comes to developing his natural talents with play.

dog walk those three steps without pulling on the lead. Once he will walk calmly beside you for three steps without pulling, increase the number of steps you take to five. When he will walk politely beside you while you take five steps, you can increase the length of your walk to ten steps. Keep increasing the length of your stroll until the dog will walk quietly beside you without pulling as long as you want him to heel. When you stop heeling, indicate to the dog that the exercise is over by verbally praising as you pet him and say "OK, good dog." The "OK" is used as a release word, meaning that the exercise is finished and the dog is free to relax.

If you are dealing with a dog who insists on pulling you around, simply "put on your brakes" and stand your ground

until the dog realizes that the two of you are not going anywhere until he is beside you and moving at your pace, not his. It may take some time just standing there to convince the dog that you are the leader and that you will be the one to decide on the direction and speed of your travel.

Each time the dog looks up at you or slows down to give a slack lead between the two of you, quietly praise him and say "Good heel. Good dog." Eventually, the dog will begin to respond and within a few days he will be walking politely beside you without pulling on the lead. At first, the training sessions should be kept short and very positive; soon the dog will be able to walk nicely with you for increasingly longer distances. Remember also to give the dog free time and the opportunity to run and play when you have finished heel practice.

WEANING OFF FOOD IN TRAINING

Food is used in training new behaviors. Once the dog understands what behavior goes with a specific command, it is time to start weaning him off the food treats. At first, give a treat after each exercise. Then, start to give a treat only after every other exercise. Mix up the times when you offer a food reward and the times when you only offer praise so that the dog will never know when he is going to receive both food and praise and when he is going to receive only praise. This is called a variable-ratio reward system. It proves successful because there is always the chance that the owner will produce a treat, so the dog never stops trying for that reward. No matter what, *always* give verbal praise.

OBEDIENCE CLASSES
It is a good idea to enroll in an obedience class if one is available in your area. If yours is a show dog, classes to prepare both of you for the ring would be more appropriate. Many areas have dog clubs that offer basic obedience training as well as preparatory classes for obedience competition. There are also local dog trainers who offer similar classes.

At obedience events, dogs can earn titles at various levels of competition. The beginning levels of obedience competition include basic behaviors such as sit, down, heel, etc. The more advanced levels of competition include jumping, retrieving, scent discrimination and signal work. The advanced levels require a dog and owner to put a lot of time and effort into their training. The titles that can be earned at these levels of competition are very prestigious.

A BORN PRODIGY
Occasionally, a dog and owner who have not attended formal classes have been able to earn entry-level obedience titles by obtaining competition rules and regulations from a local kennel club and practicing on their own to a degree of perfection. Obtaining the higher level titles, however, almost always requires extensive training under the tutelage of experienced instructors. In addition, the more difficult levels require more specialized equipment whereas the lower levels do not.

FIELD TRAINING

The modern Chesapeake Bay Retriever retains his reputation as the paragon of duck dogs, the ultimate in loyalty and bravery, and the only possible choice for the true waterfowler. His enduring traits of strength, insatiable love of water, single-minded devotion to retrieving birds, intense loyalty and steadfast possessiveness are still hallmarks of the breed two centuries after Sailor and Canton were first rescued off the coast of Maryland.

This dog is what he appears to be—a rugged, built-to-work

Retrieving birds and the water are two of the Chesapeake's favorite things in the world. Field training requires time and commitment for the Chessie to hone his innate skills.

> **HELPING PAWS**
> Your dog may not be the next Lassie, but every pet has the potential to do some tricks well. Identify his natural talents and hone them. Is your dog always happy and upbeat? Teach him to wag his tail or give you his paw on command. Real homebodies can be trained to do household chores, such as carrying dirty laundry or retrieving the morning paper.

water dog. A large dog according to the standard, yet his size is overshadowed by his heart, courage and his drive. His woolly undercoat is designed for warmth, allowing him to work in icy waters, and, in fact, relish every moment. He will charge after ducks in the water and geese in the cornfields, and plunge through ice and muck for either. The Chessie's superior nose allows him to work close without pushing the birds ahead. Although his versatility allows him to live happily in the home without a hunting career, the true Chessie heart eagerly beats at the very prospect of retrieving.

The current retriever world offers several venues where the Chesapeake can pursue the sport that he loves best. For example, the American Kennel Club sponsors field trials in which dogs compete for championship points to earn the titles of Field Champion and Amateur Field Champion. For the non-competitive sportsman, the AKC also sponsors hunting tests, which involve simulated hunting situations that test the dog's natural ability, awarding suffix titles for qualifying scores. Chesapeake breed clubs also host Working Dog tests, smaller-scale retrieving events where owners and handlers can earn working titles proffered by the national breed club.

Training a Chesapeake for field work and competition is best handled by the dog's owner whenever possible. Because of his intense loyalty to his master and his aversion to heavy-handed training, most Chessies do not thrive or learn readily with a professional trainer. Indeed, many professionals have training programs that are not compatible with the Chessie's unique person-

ality, and most professionals are unwilling, or at best unenthusiastic, about working with a retriever known to be stubborn and independent. The best course is to train your own dog with one or more experienced Chesapeake hunters to achieve the maximum response from the dog.

Although not bred as a herding dog, the Chessie can be taught to perform almost any task. This dog has learned to keep his small flock together on the farm.

OTHER ACTIVITIES FOR LIFE

There are many activities that can bring fun and rewards to both owner and dog once they have mastered basic obedience. Teaching the dog to help out around the home, in the yard or on the farm provides great satisfaction to both dog and owner. In addition, the dog's help makes life a little easier for his owner and raises his stature as a valued companion to his family. It helps give the dog a purpose by occupying his mind and providing an outlet for his energy.

Backpacking is an exciting and healthy activity that the dog

OBEDIENCE SCHOOL

A basic obedience beginner's class usually lasts for six to eight weeks. Dog and owner attend an hour-long lesson once a week and practice for a few minutes, several times a day, each day at home. If done properly, the whole procedure will result in a well-mannered dog and an owner who delights in living with a pet that is eager to please and enjoys doing things with his owner.

can be taught without assistance from more than his owner. The exercise of walking and climbing is good for man and dog alike, and the bond that they develop together is priceless. The rule for backpacking with any dog is never to expect the dog to carry more than one-sixth of his body weight.

If you are interested in participating in organized competition with your Chesapeake other than obedience or field events, agility is something in which you and your dog can become involved once he has reached the appropriate age to begin training. Agility is a popular sport in which dogs run through an obstacle course that includes

In full flight, this Chessie has retrieved a downed bird and is swiftly returning it to the hunter.

> **FETCH!**
> Play fetching games with your puppy in an enclosed area where he can retrieve his toy and bring it back to you. Always use a toy or object designated just for this purpose. Never use a shoe, sock or other item he may later confuse with those in your closet or underneath your chair.

various jumps, tunnels and other exercises to test the dog's speed and coordination. The owners run beside their dogs to give commands and to guide the dogs through the course. Although competitive, the focus is on fun— it's fun to do, fun to watch and great exercise.

CHESAPEAKE BAY RETRIEVER

Dogs suffer from many of the same physical illnesses as people and might even share many of the same psychological problems. Since people usually know more about human diseases than canine maladies, many of the terms used in this chapter will be familiar but not necessarily those used by veterinarians. For example, we will use the familiar term *x-ray* instead of *radiograph*. We will also use the familiar term *symptoms*, even though dogs don't have symptoms, which are verbal descriptions of something the patient feels or observes himself that he regards as abnormal. Dogs have *clinical signs* since they cannot speak, so we have to look for these clinical signs…but we still use the term *symptoms* in the book.

Medicine is a constantly changing art, of course with scientific input as well. Things alter as we learn more and more about basic sciences such as genetics and biochemistry, and have use of more sophisticated imaging techniques like Computer Aided Tomography (CAT scans) or Magnetic Resonance Imaging (MRI

scans). There is academic dispute about many canine maladies, so different veterinarians treat them in different ways. For example, some vets have a greater emphasis on surgical techniques than others.

SELECTING A QUALIFIED VET
Your selection of a veterinarian should be based on personal recommendation for his skills with dogs; if possible, specifically the retriever breeds. If the vet is based nearby, it will be helpful because you might have an emergency or need to make multiple visits for treatments.

All veterinarians are licensed and should be capable of dealing with medical issues such as infections, injuries, the promotion of health (for example, by vaccination) and routine surgeries. If the problem affecting your dog is more complex, your vet will refer your pet to someone with a more detailed knowledge of what is wrong. This will usually be a specialist who concentrates in the field relevant to your dog's problem, such as a veterinary dermatology, veterinary

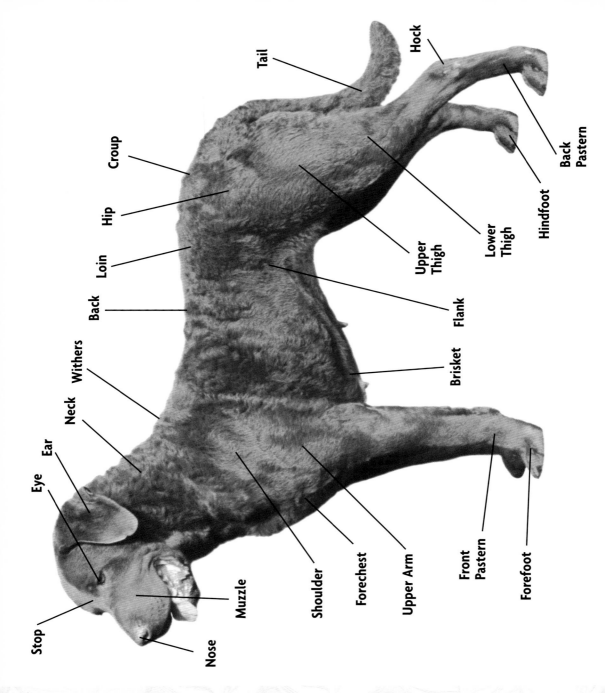

PHYSICAL STRUCTURE OF THE CHESAPEAKE BAY RETRIEVER

ophthalmology, veterinary onocology, etc.

Veterinary procedures are very costly and, as the treatments available improve, they are going to become more expensive. It is quite acceptable to discuss matters of cost with your vet; if there is more than one treatment option, cost may be a factor in deciding which route to take. It also is acceptable to get a second opinion, although it is courteous to advise the vets concerned.

Insurance against veterinary cost is becoming very popular. Investigate the various types of insurance available, as policies can range from those for emergencies only to those that cover aspects of your dog's routine health care.

PREVENTATIVE MEDICINE

It is much easier, less costly and more effective to practice preventative medicine than to fight bouts of illness and disease. Properly bred puppies of all breeds come from parents that were selected based upon their genetic-disease profiles. The puppies' dam should have been vaccinated, free of all internal and external parasites and properly nourished. For these reasons, a visit to the veterinarian who cared for the dam is recommended if at all possible. The dam passes disease resistance to her puppies, which should last from eight to ten weeks.

Breakdown of Veterinary Income by Category

2%	Dentistry
4%	Radiology
12%	Surgery
15%	Vaccinations
19%	Laboratory
23%	Examinations
25%	Medicines

A typical vet's income, categorized according to services performed. This survey dealt with small-animal (pet) practices.

Unfortunately, she can also pass on parasites and infection. This is why knowledge about her health is useful in learning more about the health of the puppies.

WEANING TO BRINGING PUPPY HOME
Puppies should be weaned by the time they are two months old. A puppy that remains for at least eight weeks with his mother and littermates usually adapts better to other dogs and people later in life.

Some new owners have their puppy examined by a vet immediately, which is a good idea unless the puppy is overtired by a long journey home from the breeder. In that case, an appointment should be made for the next day.

The puppy will have his teeth examined and have his skeletal conformation and general health checked prior to certification by the veterinarian. Puppies in

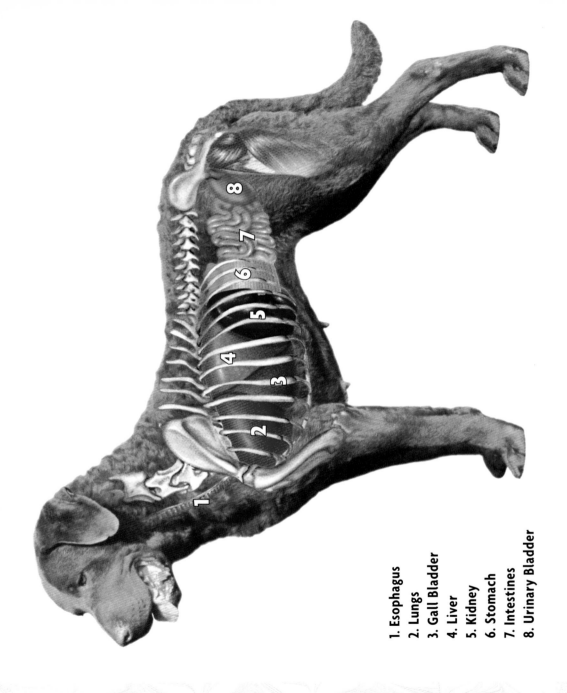

1. Esophagus
2. Lungs
3. Gall Bladder
4. Liver
5. Kidney
6. Stomach
7. Intestines
8. Urinary Bladder

INTERNAL ORGANS OF THE CHESAPEAKE BAY RETRIEVER

certain breeds have problems with their kneecaps, cataracts and other eye problems, heart murmurs and undescended testicles. Your vet might also have training in temperament evaluation. At the first visit, your vet will set up your pup's vaccination schedule.

VACCINATIONS

Most vaccinations are given by injection and should only be given by a veterinarian. Both he and you should keep a record of the date of the injection, the identification of the vaccine and the amount given. Some vets give a first vaccination at six weeks, but most dog breeders prefer the course not to commence until about eight weeks because of the risk of interaction with the antibodies produced by the dam. The vaccination schedule is usually based on a two- to four-week cycle. You must take your vet's advice as to when to vaccinate, as this may differ according to the vaccine used.

The usual vaccines contain immunizing doses of several different viruses such as distemper, parvovirus, parainfluenza and hepatitis. There are other vaccines available when the puppy is at risk. You should rely upon professional advice. This is

HEALTH AND VACCINATION SCHEDULE

AGE IN WEEKS:	6TH	8TH	10TH	12TH	14TH	16TH	20-24TH	52ND
Worm Control	✔	✔	✔	✔	✔	✔	✔	
Neutering							✔	
Heartworm		✔		✔		✔	✔	
Parvovirus	✔		✔		✔		✔	✔
Distemper		✔		✔		✔		✔
Hepatitis		✔		✔		✔		✔
Leptospirosis								✔
Parainfluenza	✔		✔		✔			✔
Dental Examination		✔					✔	✔
Complete Physical		✔					✔	✔
Coronavirus				✔			✔	✔
Canine Cough	✔							
Hip Dysplasia							✔	
Rabies							✔	

Vaccinations are not instantly effective. It takes about two weeks for the dog's immune system to develop antibodies. Most vaccinations require annual booster shots. Your veterinarian should guide you in this regard.

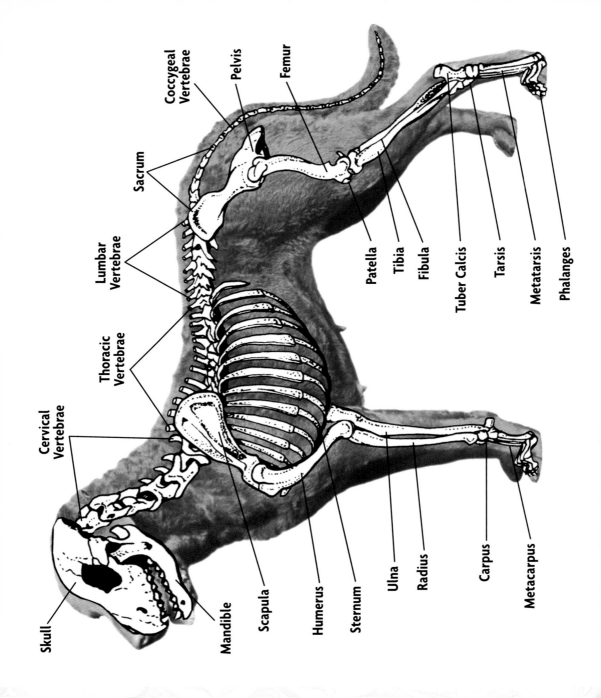

SKELETAL STRUCTURE OF THE CHESAPEAKE BAY RETRIEVER

especially true for the booster immunizations. Most vaccination programs require a booster when the puppy is a year old and once a year thereafter. In some cases, circumstances may require more or less frequent immunizations.

Canine cough, more formally known as tracheobronchitis, is immunized against with a vaccine that is sprayed into the dog's nostrils. Canine cough is usually included in routine vaccination, but it is often not as effective as the vaccines for other major diseases.

FIVE MONTHS TO ONE YEAR OF AGE
Unless you intend to breed or show your dog, neutering the puppy around six months of age is recommended. Discuss this with your veterinarian. Neutering/ spaying has proven to be extremely beneficial to male and female dogs, respectively. Besides eliminating the possibility of pregnancy and pyometra in bitches and testicular cancer in males, it greatly reduces the risk of (but does not prevent) breast cancer in bitches and prostate cancer in males.

DISEASE REFERENCE CHART

	What is it?	What causes it?	Symptoms
Leptospirosis	Severe disease that affects the internal organs; can be spread to people.	A bacterium, which is often carried by rodents, that enters through mucous membranes and spreads quickly throughout the body.	Range from fever, vomiting and loss of appetite in less severe cases to shock, irreversible kidney damage and possibly death in most severe cases.
Rabies	Potentially deadly virus that infects warm-blooded mammals.	Bite from a carrier of the virus, mainly wild animals.	1st stage: dog exhibits change in behavior, fear. 2nd stage: dog's behavior becomes more aggressive. 3rd stage: loss of coordination, trouble with bodily functions.
Parvovirus	Highly contagious virus, potentially deadly.	Ingestion of the virus, which is usually spread through the feces of infected dogs.	Most common: severe diarrhea. Also vomiting, fatigue, lack of appetite.
Canine cough	Contagious respiratory infection.	Combination of types of bacteria and virus. Most common: *Bordetella bronchiseptica* bacteria and parainfluenza virus.	Chronic cough.
Distemper	Disease primarily affecting respiratory and nervous system.	Virus that is related to the human measles virus.	Mild symptoms such as fever, lack of appetite and mucus secretion progress to evidence of brain damage, "hard pad."
Hepatitis	Virus primarily affecting the liver.	Canine adenovirus type I (CAV-1). Enters system when dog breathes in particles.	Lesser symptoms include listlessness, diarrhea, vomiting. More severe symptoms include "blue-eye" (clumps of virus in eye).
Coronavirus	Virus resulting in digestive problems.	Virus is spread through infected dog's feces.	Stomach upset evidenced by lack of appetite, vomiting, diarrhea.

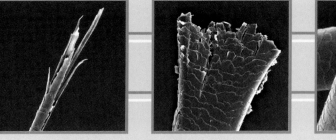
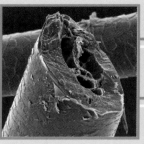

Normal hairs of a dog enlarged 200 times original size. The cuticle (outer covering) is clean and healthy. Unlike human hair that grows from the base, a dog's hair also grows from the end. Damaged hairs and split ends, illustrated above.

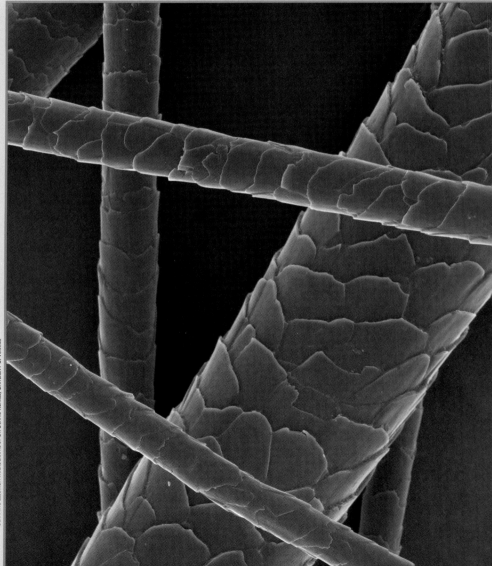

Your veterinarian should provide your puppy with a thorough dental evaluation at six months of age, ascertaining whether all of the permanent teeth have erupted properly. A home dental-care regimen should be initiated at six months, including brushing weekly and providing good dental devices (such as nylon bones). Regular dental care promotes healthy teeth, fresh breath and a longer life.

DOGS OLDER THAN ONE YEAR

Continue to visit the veterinarian at least once a year. There is no such disease as "old age," but bodily functions do change with age. The eyes and ears are no longer as efficient. Liver, kidney and intestinal functions often decline. Proper dietary changes, recommended by your veterinarian, can make life more pleasant for your aging Chesapeake and you.

SKIN PROBLEMS

Veterinarians are consulted by dog owners for skin problems more than for any other group of diseases or maladies. A dog's skin is as sensitive, if not more so, than human skin, and both can suffer from almost the same ailments (though the occurrence of acne in most breeds is rare). For this reason, veterinary dermatology has developed into a specialty practiced by many veterinarians.

Since many skin problems have visual symptoms that are almost identical, it requires the skill of an experienced veterinary dermatologist to identify and cure many of the more severe skin disorders. Pet shops sell many treatments for skin problems, but most of the treatments are directed at the symptoms and not at the underlying problem(s). If your dog is suffering from a skin disorder, you should seek professional assistance as quickly as possible. As with all diseases, the earlier a problem is identified and treated, the more likely it is that the cure will be successful.

HEREDITARY SKIN DISORDERS

Veterinary dermatologists are currently researching a number of skin disorders that are believed to have hereditary bases. These inherited diseases are transmitted by both parents, who appear (phenotypically) normal but have a recessive gene for the disease, meaning that they carry, but are not affected by, the disease. These diseases pose serious problems to breeders because in some instances there are no methods of identifying carriers. Often the secondary diseases associated with these conditions are even more debilitating than the skin disorders themselves, including cancers and respiratory problems.

Among the hereditary skin disorders, for which the mode of inheritance is known, are acrodermatitis, cutaneous asthenia (Ehlers-Danlos syndrome), sebaceous adenitis, cyclic hematopoiesis, dermatomyositis, IgA deficiency, color dilution alopecia and nodular dermatofibrosis. Some of these disorders are limited to one or two breeds, while others affect a large number of breeds. All inherited diseases must be diagnosed and treated by a veterinary specialist.

PARASITE BITES

Many of us are allergic to insect bites. The bites itch, erupt and may even become infected. Dogs have the same reaction to fleas, ticks and/or mites. When an insect lands on you, you have the chance to whisk it away with your hand. Unfortunately, when a dog is bitten by a flea, tick or mite, he can only scratch it away or bite it. By the time the dog has been bitten, the parasite has done some of its damage. It may also have laid eggs, which will cause further problems in the near future. The itching from parasite bites is probably due to the saliva injected into the site when the parasite sucks the dog's blood.

AIRBORNE ALLERGIES

Just as humans suffer from hay fever during the pollinating season, many dogs suffer from the same allergies. When the pollen count is high, your dog might suffer, but don't expect him to sneeze and have a runny nose as a human would. Dogs react to pollen allergies in the same way they react to fleas—they scratch and bite themselves.

Dogs, like humans, can be tested for allergens. Discuss the testing with your veterinarian.

ACRAL LICK GRANULOMA

Many large dogs have a very poorly understood syndrome called acral lick granuloma. The manifestation of the problem is the dog's tireless attack at a specific area of the body, almost always the legs or paws. The dog licks so intensively that he removes the hair and skin, leaving an ugly, large wound. Tiny protuberances, which are outgrowths of new capillaries, bead on the surface of the

Outdoor dogs like Chessies who work in the field and in water have many opportunities to encounter allergens, parasites and the like.

First Aid at a Glance

Burns
Place the affected area under cool water; use ice if only a small area is burnt.

Bee stings/Insect bites
Apply ice to relieve swelling; antihistamine dosed properly.

Animal bites
Clean any bleeding area; apply pressure until bleeding subsides; go to the vet.

Spider bites
Use cold compress and a pressurized pack to inhibit venom's spreading.

Antifreeze poisoning
Induce vomiting with hydrogen peroxide. Seek *immediate* veterinary help!

Fish hooks
Removal best handled by vet; hook must be cut in order to remove.

Snake bites
Pack ice around bite; contact vet quickly; identify snake for proper antivenin.

Car accident
Move dog from roadway with blanket; seek veterinary aid.

Shock
Calm the dog; keep him warm; seek immediate veterinary help.

Nosebleed
Apply cold compress to the nose; apply pressure to any visible abrasion.

Bleeding
Apply pressure above the area; treat wound by applying a cotton pack.

Heat stroke
Submerge dog in cold bath; cool down with fresh air and water; go to the vet.

Frostbite/Hypothermia
Warm the dog with a warm bath, electric blankets or hot water bottles.

Abrasions
Clean the wound and wash out thoroughly with fresh water; apply antiseptic.

 Remember: an injured dog may attempt to bite a helping hand from fear and confusion. Always muzzle the dog before trying to offer assistance.

wound. Owners who notice their dogs' biting and chewing at their extremities should have the vet determine the cause. If lick granuloma is identified, although there is no absolute cure, corticosteroids are the most common treatment.

AUTO-IMMUNE ILLNESSES

An auto-immune illness is one in which the immune system overacts and does not recognize parts of the affected person (or dog); rather, the immune system starts to react as if these parts were foreign and need to be destroyed. An example is rheumatoid arthritis, which occurs when the body does not recognize the joints, thus leading to a very painful and damaging reaction in the joints. This has nothing to do with age, so can occur in children and young dogs. The wear-and-tear arthritis of the older person or dog is osteo-arthritis.

Lupus is an auto-immune disease that affects dogs as well as people. It can take variable forms, affecting the kidneys, bones and the skin. It can be fatal, so is treated with steroids, which can themselves have very significant side effects. The steroids calm down the allergic reaction to the body's tissues, which helps the lupus, but steroids also decrease the body's reaction to real foreign substances such as bacteria, and also thin the skin and bone.

FOOD PROBLEMS

FOOD ALLERGIES

Dogs can be allergic to many foods that are best-sellers and highly recommended by breeders and veterinarians. Changing the brand of food that you buy may not eliminate the problem if the element to which the dog is allergic is contained in the new brand.

Recognizing a food allergy can be difficult. Humans often have rashes when they eat foods to which they are allergic, or have

---

A SKUNKY PROBLEM

Have you noticed your dog dragging his rump along the floor? If so, it is likely that his anal sacs are impacted or possibly infected. The anal sacs are small pouches located on both sides of the anus under the skin and muscles. They are about the size and shape of a grape and contain a foul-smelling liquid. Their contents are usually emptied when the dog has a bowel movement but, if not emptied completely, they will impact, which will cause your dog much pain. Fortunately, your veterinarian can tend to this problem easily by draining the sacs for the dog. Be aware that your dog might also empty his anal sacs in cases of extreme fright.

swelling of the lips or eyes. Dogs do not usually develop rashes, but react in the same way as they do to airborne or bite allergies—they itch, scratch and bite. While pollen allergies and parasite bites are usually seasonal, pollen allergies are year-round problems.

TREATING FOOD ALLERGY
Diagnosis of food allergy is based on a two- to four-week dietary trial with a home-cooked diet fed to the exclusion of all other foods. The diet should consist of boiled rice or potato with a source of protein that the dog has never eaten before, such as fresh or frozen fish, lamb or even something as exotic as pheasant. Water has to be the only drink, and it is really important that no other foods are fed during this trial. If the dog's condition improves, you will need to try the original diet once again to see if the itching resumes. If it does, then this confirms the diagnosis that the dog is allergic to his original diet. The treatment is long-term

feeding of something that does not distress the dog's skin, which may be in the form of one of the commercially available hypoallergenic diets or the home-made diet that you created for the allergy trial.

FOOD INTOLERANCE
Food intolerance is the inability of the dog to completely digest certain foods. This occurs because the dog does not have the chemicals necessary to digest some foodstuffs. These chemicals are called enzymes. All puppies have the enzymes necessary to digest canine milk, but some dogs do not have the enzymes to digest a very different form of milk that is commonly found in human households—milk from cows. In such dogs, drinking cows' milk results in loose bowels, stomach pains and the passage of gas.

Dogs often do not have the enzymes to digest soya or other beans. The treatment is to exclude the foodstuffs that upset your Chesapeake's digestion.

BLOAT OR GASTRIC TORSION
This is a problem found in the large, deep-chested breeds and is the subject of much research, but still manages to take away many dogs before their time and in a very horrible way.

By examining the limited support structure of a dog's stomach, it is easy to see that the stomach can

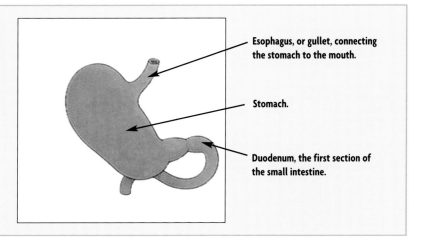

The stomach hangs like a handbag with both straps broken within the dog's deep body cavity. Support is provided by the junction with the esophagus and the junction with the duodenum.

Esophagus, or gullet, connecting the stomach to the mouth.

Stomach.

Duodenum, the first section of the small intestine.

move around easily. Those breeds with the deepest chests are at the greatest risk of having their whole stomachs twist around (gastric torsion). This cuts off the blood supply and prevents the stomach's contents from leaving, and increases the amount of gas in the stomach. Once these things have happened, surgery is vital. If the blood supply has been cut off too long and a bit of the stomach wall dies, death of the Chesapeake is almost inevitable.

The horrendous pain of this condition is due to the stomach wall's being stretched by the gas caught in the stomach, as well as

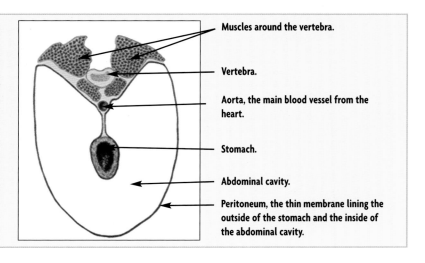

Aside from the support provided by the junction with the esophagus, or gullet, and the support provided by the junction with the first part of the small intestine, the "broken straps of the handbag," the only other support is from a thin layer of partially opaque "internal skin" called the peritoneum. No wonder the stomach can move around easily, and those breeds with the deepest chests are at the greatest risk.

Muscles around the vertebra.

Vertebra.

Aorta, the main blood vessel from the heart.

Stomach.

Abdominal cavity.

Peritoneum, the thin membrane lining the outside of the stomach and the inside of the abdominal cavity.

the stomach wall's desperately needing the blood that cannot get to it. There is the pain of not being able to pass a much greater than normal amount of wind; added to this is a pain equivalent to that of a heart attack, which is due to the heart's being starved of blood.

How to Prevent Bloat

Here are some tips on how to reduce the risk of bloat in your Chesapeake:

- Wait at least an hour after exercising your Chesapeake before feeding;
- Wait at least an hour after feeding your Chessie before exercising him;
- Feed the dog when he is calm, not nervous or excited;
- Do not feed cheap food with high cereal content;
- Feed high-quality, low-residue diets;
- Elevate food and water bowls to try to reduce any air swallowed;
- Never let your dog gulp water;
- If your Chesapeake is greedy and eats quickly, reduce the air swallowed by putting something large and inedible in the food bowl so that the dog has to pick around the object and thus eat more slowly.

Detecting Bloat

The following are symptoms of bloat and require immediate veterinary attention:

- Your dog's stomach starts to distend, ending up large and as tight as a football;
- Your dog is dribbling, as no saliva can be swallowed;
- Your dog makes frequent attempts to vomit but cannot bring anything up due to the stomach's being closed off;
- Your dog is distressed from pain;
- Your dog starts to suffer from clinical shock, meaning that there is not enough blood in the dog's circulation as the hard, dilated stomach stops the blood from returning to the heart to be pumped around the body. Clinical shock is indicated by pale gums and tongue, as they have been starved of blood. The shocked dog also has glazed, staring eyes.

You have minutes, yes *minutes*, to get your dog into surgery. If you see any of these symptoms at any time of the day or night, get to the vet's clinic immediately, as that is where all the equipment is located. Someone will have to phone and warn that you are on your way (which is a justification for the invention of the cellular phone!), so that they can be prepared to get your pet on the operating table.

It is possible for a dog to have more than one incident of gastric torsion, even if he has had his stomach stapled, in which the stomach is stapled to the inside of the chest wall to give extra support and prevent its twisting.

A male dog flea, *Ctenocephalides canis.*

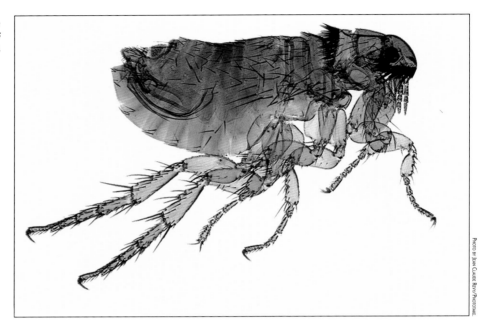

PHOTO BY JEAN CLAUDE REVY/PHOTOTAKE

EXTERNAL PARASITES

FLEAS

Of all the problems to which dogs are prone, none is more well known and frustrating than fleas. Flea infestation is relatively simple to cure but difficult to prevent. Parasites that are harbored inside the body are a bit more difficult to eradicate but they are easier to control.

To control flea infestation, you have to understand the flea's life cycle. Fleas are often thought of as a summertime problem, but centrally heated homes have changed the patterns and fleas can be found at any time of the year. The most effective method of flea control is a two-stage approach: one stage to kill the adult fleas, and the other to control the development of pre-adult fleas. Unfortunately, no single active ingredient is effective against all stages of the life cycle.

FLEA KILLER CAUTION— "POISON"

Flea-killers are poisonous. You should not spray these toxic chemicals on areas of a dog's body that he licks, including his genitals and his face. Flea killers taken internally are a better answer, but check with your vet in case internal therapy is not advised for your dog.

LIFE CYCLE STAGES

During its life, a flea will pass through four life stages: egg, larva, pupa or nymph and adult. The adult stage is the most visible and irritating stage of the flea life cycle, and this is why the majority of flea-control products concentrate on this stage. The fact is that adult fleas account for only 1% of the total flea population, and the other 99% exist in pre-adult stages, i.e., eggs, larvae and nymphs. The pre-adult stages are barely visible to the naked eye.

THE LIFE CYCLE OF THE FLEA

Eggs are laid on the dog, usually in quantities of about 20 or 30, several times a day. The adult female flea must have a blood meal before each egg-laying session. When first laid, the eggs will cling to the dog's hair, as the eggs are still moist. However, they will quickly dry out and fall from the dog, especially if the dog moves around or scratches. Many eggs will fall off in the dog's favorite area or an area in which he spends a lot of time, such as his bed.

Once the eggs fall from the dog onto the carpet or furniture, they will hatch into larvae. This takes from one to ten days. Larvae are not particularly mobile and will usually travel only a few inches from where they hatch. However, they do have a tendency to move away from bright light and heavy

EN GARDE:
CATCHING FLEAS OFF GUARD!
Consider the following ways to arm yourself against fleas:
- Add a small amount of pennyroyal or eucalyptus oil to your dog's bath. These natural remedies repel fleas.
- Supplement your dog's food with fresh garlic (minced or grated) and a hearty amount of brewer's yeast, both of which ward off fleas.
- Use a flea comb on your dog daily. Submerge fleas in a cup of bleach to kill them quickly.
- Confine the dog to only a few rooms to limit the spread of fleas in the home.
- Vacuum daily...and get all of the crevices! Dispose of the bag every few days until the problem is under control.
- Wash your dog's bedding daily. Cover cushions where your dog sleeps with towels, and wash the towels often.

traffic—under furniture and behind doors are common places to find high quantities of flea larvae.

The flea larvae feed on dead organic matter, including adult flea feces, until they are ready to change into adult fleas. Fleas will usually remain as larvae for around seven days. After this period, the larvae will pupate into protective pupae. While inside the pupae, the larvae will undergo metamorphosis and change into adult fleas. This can take as little time as a few days, but the adult fleas can remain inside the pupae waiting to hatch for up to two years. The pupae are signaled to hatch by certain stimuli, such as physical pressure—the pupae's being stepped on, heat from an animal's lying on the pupae or increased carbon-dioxide levels and vibrations—indicating that a suitable host is available.

Once hatched, the adult flea must feed within a few days. Once the adult flea finds a host, it will not leave voluntarily. It only becomes dislodged by grooming or the host animal's scratching. The adult flea will remain on the

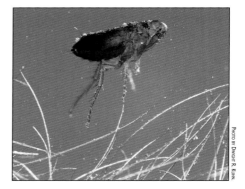

host for the duration of its life unless forcibly removed.

TREATING THE ENVIRONMENT AND THE DOG

Treating fleas should be a two-pronged attack. First, the environment needs to be treated; this includes carpets and furniture, especially the dog's bedding and areas underneath furniture. The environment should be treated with a household spray containing an Insect Growth Regulator (IGR) and an insecticide to kill the adult fleas. Most IGRs are effective against eggs and larvae; they actually mimic the fleas' own hormones and stop the eggs and larvae from developing into adult fleas. There are currently no treatments available to attack the pupa stage of the life cycle, so the adult insecticide is used to kill the newly hatched adult fleas before they find a host. Most IGRs are active for many months, while adult insecticides are only active for a few days.

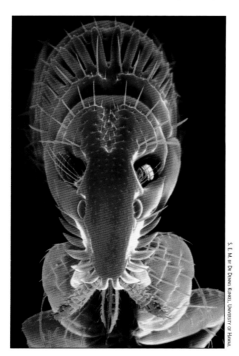

A scanning electron micrograph of a dog or cat flea, *Ctenocephalides*, magnified more than 100x. This image has been colorized for effect.

THE LIFE CYCLE OF THE FLEA

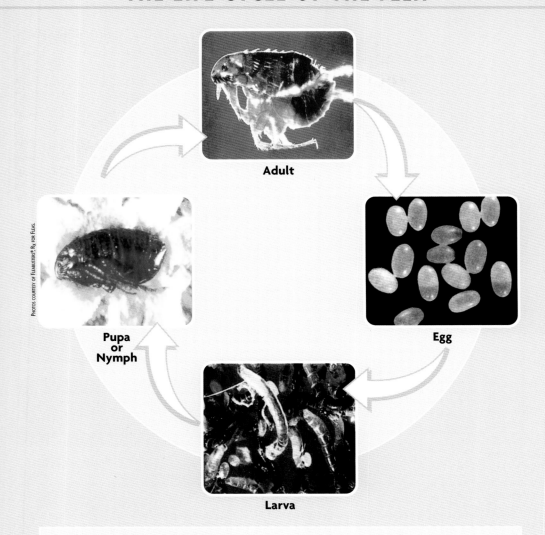

Adult

Egg

Larva

Pupa
or
Nymph

Fleas have been around for millions of years and have adapted to changing host animals. They are able to go through a complete life cycle in less than one month or they can extend their lives to almost two years by remaining as pupae or cocoons. They do not need blood or any other food for up to 20 months.

> ## INSECT GROWTH REGULATOR (IGR)
>
> Two types of products should be used when treating fleas—a product to treat the pet and a product to treat the home. Adult fleas represent less than 1% of the flea population. The pre-adult fleas (eggs, larvae and pupae) represent more than 99% of the flea population and are found in the environment; it is in the case of pre-adult fleas that products containing an Insect Growth Regulator (IGR) should be used in the home.
>
> IGRs are a new class of compounds used to prevent the development of insects. They do not kill the insect outright, but instead use the insect's biology against it to stop it from completing its growth. Products that contain methoprene are the world's first and leading IGRs. Used to control fleas and other insects, this type of IGR will stop flea larvae from developing and protect the house for up to seven months.

The American dog tick, *Dermacentor variabilis*, is probably the most common tick found on dogs. Look at the strength in its eight legs! No wonder it's hard to detach them.

When treating with a household spray, it is a good idea to vacuum before applying the product. This stimulates as many pupae as possible to hatch into adult fleas. The vacuum cleaner should also be treated with an insecticide to prevent the eggs and larvae that have been collected in the vacuum bag from hatching.

The second stage of treatment is to apply an adult insecticide to the dog. Traditionally, this would be in the form of a collar or a spray, but more recent innovations include digestible insecticides that poison the fleas when they ingest the dog's blood. Alternatively, there are drops that, when placed on the back of the dog's neck, spread throughout the hair and skin to kill adult fleas.

Ticks

Though not as common as fleas, ticks are found all over the tropical and temperate world. They don't bite, like fleas; they harpoon. They dig their sharp proboscis (nose) into the dog's skin and drink the blood. Their only food and drink is dog's blood. Dogs can get Lyme

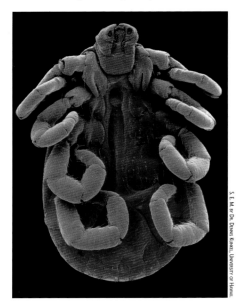

S.E.M. by Dr. Dennis Kunkel, University of Hawaii

disease, Rocky Mountain spotted fever, tick bite paralysis and many other diseases from ticks. They may live where fleas are found and they like to hide in cracks or seams in walls. They are controlled the same way fleas are controlled.

The American dog tick, *Dermacentor variabilis*, may well be the most common dog tick in many geographical areas, especially those areas where the climate is hot and humid. Most dog ticks have life expectancies of a week to six months, depending upon climatic conditions. They can neither jump nor fly, but they can crawl slowly and can range up to 16 feet to reach a sleeping or unsuspecting dog.

MITES

Just as fleas and ticks can be problematic for your dog, mites can also lead to an itchy nuisance. Microscopic in size, mites are related to ticks and generally take up permanent residence on their host animal—in this case, your dog! The term *mange* refers to any infestation caused by one of the mighty mites, of which there are six varieties that concern dog owners.

Demodex mites cause a condition known as demodicosis (sometimes called red mange or follicular mange), in which the

DEER-TICK CROSSING

The great outdoors may be fun for your dog, but it also is a home to dangerous ticks. Deer ticks carry a bacterium known as *Borrelia burgdorferi* and are most active in the autumn and spring. When infections are caught early, penicillin and tetracycline are effective antibiotics, but, if left untreated, the bacteria may cause neurological, kidney and cardiac problems as well as long-term trouble with walking and painful joints.

S. E. M. BY DR. ANDREW SPIELMAN/PHOTOTAKE.

PHOTO BY DR. DENNIS KUNKEL, UNIVERSITY OF HAWAII.

The head of an American dog tick, *Dermacentor variabilis*, enlarged and colorized for effect.

The mange mite, *Psoroptes bovis*, can infest cattle and other domestic animals.

PHOTO BY JAMES HAYDEN/YOAV/PHOTOTAKE.

mites live in the dog's hair follicles and sebaceous glands in larger-than-normal numbers. This type of mange is commonly passed from the dam to her puppies and usually shows up on the puppies' muzzles, though demodicosis is not transferable from one normal dog to another. Most dogs recover from this type of mange without any treatment, though topical therapies are commonly prescribed by the vet.

The *Cheyletiellosis* mite is the hook-mouthed culprit associated with "walking dandruff," a condition that affects dogs as well as cats and rabbits. This mite lives on the surface of the animal's skin and is readily transferable through direct or indirect contact with an affected animal. The dandruff is present in the form of scaly skin, which may or may not be itchy. If not treated, this mange can affect a whole kennel of dogs and can be spread to humans as well.

The *Sarcoptes* mite causes intense itching on the dog in the form of a condition known as scabies or sarcoptic mange. The cycle of the *Sarcoptes* mite lasts about three weeks, and the mites live in the top layer of the dog's skin (epidermis), preferably in areas with little hair. Scabies is

Human lice look like dog lice; the two are closely related.

PHOTO BY DWIGHT R. KUHN.

highly contagious and can be passed to humans. Sometimes an allergic reaction to the mite worsens the severe itching associated with sarcoptic mange.

Ear mites, *Otodectes cynotis,* lead to otodectic mange, which most commonly affects the outer ear canal of the dog, though other areas can be affected as well. Dogs with ear-mite infestation commonly scratch at their ears, causing further irritation, and shake their heads. Dark brown droppings in the outer ear confirm the diagnosis. Your vet can prescribe a treatment to flush out the ears and kill any eggs in the ears. A complete month of treatment is necessary to cure the mange.

Two other mites, less common in dogs, include *Dermanyssus gallinae* (the poultry or red mite) and *Eutrombicula alfreddugesi* (the North American mite associated with trombiculidiasis or chigger infestation). The poultry mite frequently lives on chickens, but can transfer to dogs who spend time near farm animals. Chigger infestation affects dogs in the Central US

DO NOT MIX
Never mix parasite-control products without first consulting your vet. Some products can become toxic when combined with others and can cause fatal consequences.

NOT A DROP TO DRINK
Never allow your dog to swim in polluted water or public areas where water quality can be suspect. Even perfectly clear water can harbor parasites, many of which can cause serious to fatal illnesses in canines. Areas inhabited by waterfowl and other wildlife are especially dangerous.

who have exposure to woodlands. The types of mange caused by both of these mites are treatable by vets.

INTERNAL PARASITES

Most animals—fishes, birds and mammals, including dogs and humans—have worms and other parasites that live inside their bodies. According to Dr. Herbert R. Axelrod, the fish pathologist, there are two kinds of parasites: dumb and smart. The smart parasites live in peaceful cooperation with their hosts (symbiosis), while the dumb parasites kill their hosts. Most worm infections are relatively easy to control. If they are not controlled, they weaken the host dog to the point that other medical problems occur, but they do not kill the host as dumb parasites would.

A brown dog tick, *Rhipicephalus sanguineus,* is an uncommon but annoying tick found on dogs.
PHOTO BY CAROLINA BIOLOGICAL SUPPLY/PHOTOTAKE.

Photo by Carolina Biological Supply/Phototake.

The roundworm *Rhabditis* can infect both dogs and humans.

The roundworm, *Ascaris lumbricoides*.

ROUNDWORMS

Average-size dogs can pass 1,360,000 roundworm eggs every day. For example, if there were only 1 million dogs in the world, the world would be saturated with thousands of tons of dog feces. These feces would contain around 15,000,000,000 roundworm eggs.

Up to 31% of home yards and children's sand boxes in the US contain roundworm eggs.

Flushing dog's feces down the toilet is not a safe practice because the usual sewage treatments do not destroy roundworm eggs.

Infected puppies start shedding roundworm eggs at three weeks of age. They can be infected by their mother's milk.

ROUNDWORMS

The roundworms that infect dogs are known scientifically as *Toxocara canis*. They live in the dog's intestines and shed eggs continually. It has been estimated that a dog produces about 6 or more ounces of feces every day. Each ounce of feces averages hundreds of thousands of roundworm eggs. There are no known areas in which dogs roam that do not contain roundworm eggs. The greatest danger of roundworms is that they infect people, too! It is wise to have your dog tested regularly for roundworms.

In young puppies, roundworms cause bloated bellies, diarrhea, coughing and vomiting, and are transmitted from the dam (through blood or milk). Affected puppies will not appear as animated as normal puppies. The worms appear spaghetti-like, measuring as long as 6 inches. Adult dogs can acquire roundworms through coprophagia (eating contaminated feces) or by killing rodents that carry roundworms.

Roundworm infection can kill puppies and cause severe problems in adults, as the hatched larvae travel to the lungs and trachea through the bloodstream. Cleanliness is the best preventative for roundworms. Always pick up after your dog and dispose of feces in appropriate receptacles.

Photo by Dwight R. Kuhn.

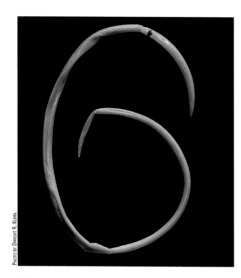

HOOKWORMS

In the United States, dog owners have to be concerned about four different species of hookworm, the most common and most serious of which is *Ancylostoma caninum,* which prefers warm climates. The others are *Ancylostoma braziliense, Ancylostoma tubaeforme* and *Uncinaria stenocephala,* the latter of which is a concern to dogs living in the Northern US and Canada, as this species prefers cold climates. Hookworms are dangerous to humans as well as to dogs and cats, and can be the cause of severe anemia due to iron deficiency. The worm uses its teeth to attach itself to the dog's intestines and changes the site of its attachment about six times per day. Each time the worm repositions itself, the dog loses blood and can become anemic. *Ancylostoma caninum* is the most likely of the four species to cause anemia in the dog.

Symptoms of hookworm infection include dark stools, weight loss, general weakness, pale coloration and anemia, as well as possible skin problems. Fortunately, hookworms are easily purged from the affected dog with a number of medications that have proven effective. Discuss these with your vet. Most heartworm preventatives include a hookworm insecticide as well.

Owners also must be aware that hookworms can infect humans, who can acquire the larvae through exposure to contaminated feces. Since the worms cannot complete their life cycle on a human, the worms simply infest the skin and cause irritation. This condition is known as cutaneous larva migrans syndrome. As a preventative, use disposable gloves or a "poop-scoop" to pick up your dog's droppings and prevent your dog (or neighborhood cats) from defecating in children's play areas.

The hookworm, *Ancylostoma caninum.*

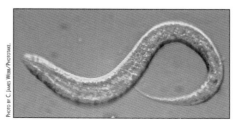

The infective stage of the hookworm larva.

TAPEWORMS

Humans, rats, squirrels, foxes, coyotes, wolves and domestic dogs are all susceptible to tapeworm infection. Except in humans, tapeworms are usually not a fatal infection. Infected individuals can harbor 1000 parasitic worms.

Tapeworms, like some other types of worm, are hermaphroditic, meaning male and female in the same worm.

If dogs eat infected rats or mice, or anything else infected with tapeworm, they get the tapeworm disease. One month after attaching to a dog's intestine, the worm starts shedding eggs. These eggs are infective immediately. Infective eggs can live for a few months without a host animal.

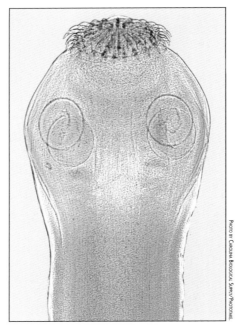

The head and rostellum (the round prominence on the scolex) of a tapeworm, which infects dogs and humans.

PHOTO BY CAROLINA BIOLOGICAL SUPPLY/PHOTOTAKE

TAPEWORMS

There are many species of tapeworm, all of which are carried by fleas! The most common tapeworm affecting dogs is known as *Dipylidium caninum*. The dog eats the flea and starts the tapeworm cycle. Humans can also be infected with tapeworms—so don't eat fleas! Fleas are so small that your dog could pass them onto your hands, your plate or your food and thus make it possible for you to ingest a flea that is carrying tapeworm eggs.

While tapeworm infection is not life-threatening in dogs (smart parasite!), it can be the cause of a very serious liver disease for humans. About 50% of the humans infected with *Echinococcus multilocularis*, a type of tapeworm that causes alveolar hydatid, perish.

WHIPWORMS

In North America, whipworms are counted among the most common parasitic worms in dogs. The whipworm's scientific name is *Trichuris vulpis*. These worms attach themselves in the lower parts of the intestine, where they feed. Affected dogs may only experience upset tummies, colic and diarrhea. These worms, however, can live for months or years in the dog, beginning their larval stage in the small intestine, spending their adult stage in the large intestine and finally passing infective eggs through the dog's feces. The only way to detect whipworms is through a fecal examination, though this is not always foolproof. Treatment for whipworms is tricky, due to the worms' unusual life-cycle pattern, and very often dogs are reinfected due to exposure to infective eggs on the ground. The whipworm eggs can survive in the environment for as long as five years; thus, cleaning up droppings in your own backyard as well as in public places is absolutely essential for sanitation purposes and the health of your dog and others.

THREADWORMS

Though less common than roundworms, hookworms and those previously mentioned, threadworms concern dog owners in the Southwestern US and Gulf Coast area where the climate is hot and humid. Living in the small intestine of the dog, this worm measures a mere 2 millimeters and is round in shape. Like that of the whipworm, the threadworm's life cycle is very complex and the eggs and larvae are passed through the feces. A deadly disease in humans, *Strongyloides* readily infects people, and the handling of feces is the most common means of transmission. Threadworms are most often seen in young puppies; bloody diarrhea and pneumonia are symptoms. Sick puppies must be isolated and treated immediately; vets recommend a follow-up treatment one month later.

HEARTWORM PREVENTATIVES

There are many heartworm preventatives on the market, many of which are sold at your veterinarian's office. These products can be given daily or monthly, depending on the manufacturer's instructions. All of these preventatives contain chemical insecticides directed at killing heartworms, which leads to some controversy among dog owners. In effect, heartworm preventatives are necessary evils, though you should determine how necessary based on your pet's lifestyle. There is no doubt that heartworm is a dreadful disease that threatens the lives of dogs. However, the likelihood of your dog's being bitten by an infected mosquito is slim in most places, and a mosquito-repellent (or an herbal remedy such as Wormwood or Black Walnut) is much safer for your dog and will not compromise his immune system (the way heartworm preventatives will). Should you decide to use the traditional preventative "medications," you can consider giving the pill every other or third month. Since the toxins in the pill will kill the heartworms at all stages of development, the pill would be effective in killing larvae, nymphs or adults, and it takes four months for the larvae to reach the adult stage. Thus, there is no rationale to poisoning the dog's system on a monthly basis. Lastly, do not give the pill during the winter months, since there are no mosquitoes around to pass on their infection, unless you live in a tropical environment.

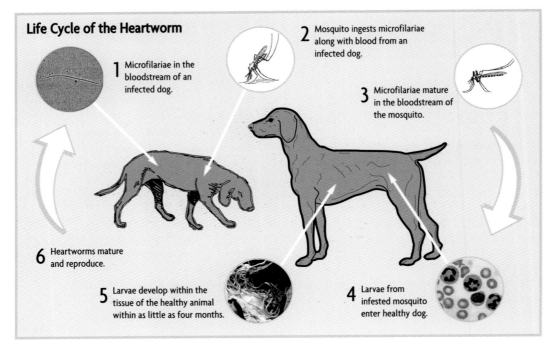

Life Cycle of the Heartworm

1 Microfilariae in the bloodstream of an infected dog.

2 Mosquito ingests microfilariae along with blood from an infected dog.

3 Microfilariae mature in the bloodstream of the mosquito.

6 Heartworms mature and reproduce.

5 Larvae develop within the tissue of the healthy animal within as little as four months.

4 Larvae from infested mosquito enter healthy dog.

HEARTWORMS

Heartworms are thin, extended worms up to 12 inches long, which live in a dog's heart and the major blood vessels surrounding it. Dogs may have up to 200 worms. Symptoms may be loss of energy, loss of appetite, coughing, the development of a pot belly and anemia.

Heartworms are transmitted by mosquitoes. The mosquito drinks the blood of an infected dog and takes in larvae with the blood. The larvae, called microfilariae, develop within the body of the mosquito and are passed on to the next dog bitten after the larvae

mature. It takes two to three weeks for the larvae to develop to the infective stage within the body of the mosquito. Dogs are usually treated at about six weeks of age and maintained on a prophylactic dose given monthly.

Blood testing for heartworms is not necessarily indicative of how seriously your dog is infected. Although this is a dangerous disease, it is not easy for a dog to be infected. Discuss the various preventatives with your vet, as there are many different types now available. Together you can decide on a safe course of prevention for your dog.

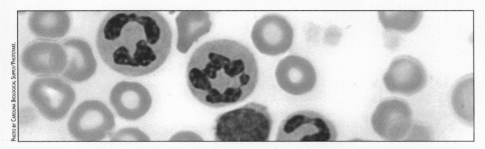

Magnified heartworm larvae, *Dirofilaria immitis*.

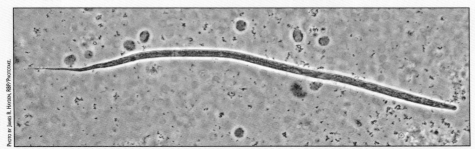

Heartworm, *Dirofilaria immitis*.

The heart of a dog infected with canine heartworm, *Dirofilaria immitis*.

HOMEOPATHY:
an alternative
to conventional
medicine

"Less is Most"

Using this principle, the strength of a homeopathic remedy is measured by the number of serial dilutions that were undertaken to create it. The greater the number of serial dilutions, the greater the strength of the homeopathic remedy. The potency of a remedy that has been made by making a dilution of 1 part in 100 parts (or 1/100) is 1c or 1cH. If this remedy is subjected to a series of further dilutions, each one being 1/100, a more dilute and stronger remedy is produced. If the remedy is diluted in this way six times, it is called 6c or 6cH. A dilution of 6c is 1 part in 1,000,000,000,000. In general, higher potencies in more frequent doses are better for acute symptoms and lower potencies in more infrequent doses are more useful for chronic, long-standing problems.

CURING OUR DOGS NATURALLY

Holistic medicine means treating the whole animal as a unique, perfect, living being. Generally, holistic treatments do not suppress the symptoms that the body naturally produces, as do most medications prescribed by conventional doctors and vets. Holistic methods seek to cure disease by regaining balance and harmony in the patient's environment. Some of these methods include use of nutritional therapy, herbs, flower essences, aromatherapy, acupuncture, massage, chiropractic and, of course, the most popular holistic approach, homeopathy.

Homeopathy is a theory or system of treating illness with small doses of substances which, if administered in larger quantities, would produce the symptoms that the patient already has. This approach is often described as "like cures like." Although modern veterinary medicine is geared toward the "quick fix," homeopathy relies on the belief that, given the time, the body is able to heal itself and return to its natural, healthy state.

Choosing a remedy to cure a problem in our dogs is the difficult part of homeopathy. Consult with your vet for a professional diagnosis of your dog's symptoms. Often these symptoms require

immediate conventional care. If your vet is willing and knowledgeable, you may attempt a homeopathic remedy. Be aware that cortisone prevents homeopathic remedies from working. There are hundreds of possibilities and combinations to cure many problems in dogs, from basic physical problems such as excessive shedding, fleas or other parasites, unattractive doggy odor, bad breath, upset tummy, obesity, dry, oily or dull coat, diarrhea, ear problems or eye discharge (including tears and dry or mucousy matter), to behavioral abnormalities such as fear of loud noises, habitual licking, poor appetite, excessive barking and various phobias. From alumina to zincum metallicum, the remedies span the planet and the imagination…from flowers and weeds to chemicals, insect droppings, diesel smoke and volcanic ash.

Using "Like to Treat Like"

Unlike conventional medicines that suppress symptoms, homeopathic remedies treat illnesses with small doses of substances that, if administered in larger quantities, would produce the symptoms that the patient already has. While the same homeopathic remedy can be used to treat different symptoms in different dogs, here are some interesting remedies and their uses.

Apis Mellifica
(made from honey bee venom) can be used for allergies or to reduce swelling that occurs in acutely infected kidneys.

Diesel Smoke
can be used to help control travel sickness.

Calcarea Fluorica
(made from calcium fluoride, which helps harden bone structure) can be useful in treating hard lumps in tissues.

Natrum Muriaticum
(made from common salt, sodium chloride) is useful in treating thin, thirsty dogs.

Nitricum Acidum
(made from nitric acid) is used for symptoms you would expect to see from contact with acids, such as lesions, especially where the skin joins the linings of body orifices or openings such as the lips and nostrils.

Symphytum
(made from the herb Knitbone, *Symphytum officianale*) is used to encourage bones to heal.

Urtica Urens
(made from the common stinging nettle) is used in treating painful, irritating rashes.

CHESAPEAKE BAY RETRIEVER

When you purchase your Chesapeake Bay Retriever, you will make it clear to the breeder whether you want one just as a lovable companion and pet, or if you hope to be buying a Chesapeake with show prospects. No reputable breeder will sell you a young puppy and tell you that it is *definitely* of show quality, for so much can go wrong during the early months of a puppy's development. If you plan to show, what you will hopefully have acquired is a puppy with "show potential."

To the novice, exhibiting a Chesapeake Bay Retriever in the show ring may look easy, but it takes a lot of hard work and devotion to do top winning at a show such as the prestigious Westminster Kennel Club dog show, not to mention a little luck, too!

The first concept that the canine novice learns when watching a dog show is that each dog first competes against members of his own breed. Once the judge has selected the best member of each breed (Best of Breed), provided that the show is judged on a Group system, that chosen dog will compete with other dogs in his group. Finally, the dogs chosen first in each group will compete for Best in Show.

The second concept that you must understand is that the dogs are not actually compared against one another. The judge compares each dog against his breed standard, the written description of the ideal specimen that is approved by the American Kennel Club (AKC). While some early breed standards were indeed based on specific dogs

---

INFORMATION ON CLUBS

You can get information about dog shows from the national kennel clubs:

American Kennel Club
5580 Centerview Dr., Raleigh, NC 27606-3390
www.akc.org

United Kennel Club
100 E. Kilgore Road, Kalamazoo, MI 49002
www.ukcdogs.com

Canadian Kennel Club
89 Skyway Ave., Suite 100, Etobicoke, Ontario
M9W 6R4, Canada
www.ckc.ca

The Kennel Club
1-5 Clarges St., Piccadilly
London W1Y 8AB, UK
www.the-kennel-club.org.uk

that were famous or popular, many dedicated enthusiasts say that a perfect specimen, as described in the standard, has never walked into a show ring, has never been bred and, to the woe of dog breeders around the globe, does not exist. Breeders attempt to get as close to this ideal as possible with every litter, but theoretically the "perfect" dog is so elusive that it is impossible. (And if the "perfect" dog were born, breeders and judges would never agree that it was indeed "perfect.")

If you are interested in exploring the world of dog showing, your best bet is to join your local breed club or the national parent club, which is the American Chesapeake Club. These clubs often host both regional and national specialties, shows only for Chesapeake Bay Retrievers, which can include conformation as well as obedience and field trials. Even if you have no intention of competing with your Chesapeake Bay Retriever, a specialty is a like a festival for lovers of the breed who congregate to share their favorite topic: Chessies! Clubs also send out newsletters, and some organize training days and seminars in order that people may learn more about their chosen breed. To locate the breed club closest to you, contact the American Kennel Club, which furnishes the rules and regulations for all of these events plus general dog registration and other basic requirements of dog ownership.

In the US, the American Kennel Club offers three kinds of conformation shows: An all-breed show (for all AKC-recognized breeds); a specialty show (for one breed only, usually sponsored by the parent club) and a Group show (for all breeds in the group).

For a dog to become an AKC champion of record, the dog must accumulate 15 points at the shows from at least three different judges, including two "majors." A "major" is defined as a three-, four- or five-point win, and the number of points per win is determined by the number of dogs entered in the show on that day. Depending on the

Competing with other members of the breed, the Chessie that is selected as Best of Breed will continue on to compete for Best in Group against the other Best of Breed dogs.

breed, the number of points that are awarded varies. More dogs are needed to rack up the points in more popular breeds, and less dogs are needed in less popular breeds.

At any dog show, only one dog and one bitch of each breed can win points. Dog showing does not offer "co-ed" classes. Dogs and bitches never compete against each other in the classes. Non-champion dogs are called "class dogs" because they compete in one of five classes. Dogs are entered in a particular class depending on age and previous show wins. To begin, there is the Puppy Class (for 6- to 9-month-olds and for 9- to 12-month-olds); this class is followed by the Novice Class (for dogs that have not won any first prizes except in the Puppy Class or three first prizes in the Novice Class and have not accumulated any points toward their champion title); the Bred-by Exhibitor Class (for dogs handled by their breeders or by one of the breeder's immediate family); the

American-bred Class (for dogs bred in the US) and the Open Class (for any dog that is not a champion).

The judge at the show begins judging the Puppy Class, first dogs and then bitches, and proceeds through the classes. The judge places his winners first through fourth in each class. In the Winners Class, the first-place winners of each class compete with one another to determine Winners Dog and Winners Bitch. The judge also places a Reserve Winners Dog and Reserve Winners Bitch, which could be awarded the points in the case of a disqualification. The Winners Dog and Winners Bitch are the two that are awarded the points for the breed, then compete with any champions of record (often called "specials") entered in the show. The judge reviews the Winners Dog, Winners Bitch and all of the champions to select his Best of Breed. The Best of Winners is selected between the Winners Dog and Winners Bitch. Were one of these two to be selected Best of Breed, he or she would automatically be named Best of Winners as

AKC GROUPS

For showing purposes, the American Kennel Club divides its recognized breeds into seven groups: Sporting Dogs, Hounds, Working Dogs, Terriers, Toys, Non-Sporting Dogs and Herding Dogs.

well. Finally the judge selects his Best of Opposite Sex to the Best of Breed winner.

At a Group show or all-breed show, the Best of Breed winners from each breed then compete against one another for Group One through Group Four. The judge compares each Best of Breed to his breed standard, and the dog that most closely lives up to the ideal for his breed is selected as Group One. Finally, all seven group winners (from the Sporting Group, Toy Group, Hound Group, etc.) compete for Best in Show.

To find out about dog shows in your area, you can subscribe to the American Kennel Club's monthly magazine, the *American Kennel Gazette* and the accompanying *Events Calendar.* You can also look in your local newspaper for advertisements for dog shows in your area or go on the Internet to the AKC's website, www.akc.org.

If your Chesapeake Bay Retriever is six months of age or older and registered with the AKC, you can enter him a dog show where the breed is offered classes. Provided that your Chesapeake does not have a disqualifying fault, he can compete. Only unaltered dogs can be entered in a dog show, so if you have spayed or neutered your Chessie, you cannot compete in conformation shows. The reason for this is simple. Dog shows are the main forum to prove which representatives in a breed are worthy of being bred. Only dogs that have achieved champi- onships—the AKC "seal of approval" for quality in pure-bred dogs—should be bred. Altered dogs, however, can participate in other AKC events such as obedience trials and the Canine Good Citizen® program.

Before you actually step into the ring, you would be well advised to sit back and observe the judge's ring procedure. If it is your first time in the ring, do not be over- anxious and run to the front of the line. It is much better to stand back and study how the exhibitor in front of you is performing. The judge asks each handler to "stack" the dog, hopefully showing the dog off to his best advantage. The judge will observe the dog from a distance and from different angles, and

This Chessie is being gaited to demonstrate his correct structure and movement to the judge.

approach the dog to check his teeth, overall structure, alertness and muscle tone, as well as consider how well the dog "conforms" to the standard. Most importantly, the judge will have the exhibitor move the dog around the ring in some pattern that he should specify (another advantage to not going first, but always listen since some judges change their directions—and the judge is always right!). Finally, the judge will give the dog one last look before moving on to the next exhibitor.

If you are not in the top four in your class at your first show, do not be discouraged. Be patient and consistent, and you may eventually find yourself in a winning line-up. Remember that the winners were once in your shoes and have devoted many hours and much money to earn the placement. If you find that your dog is losing every time and never getting a nod, it may be time to consider a different dog sport or to just enjoy your Chessie as a pet. Parent clubs offer other events, such as agility, field events, obedience, instinct tests and more, which may be of interest to the owner of a well-trained Chesapeake Bay Retriever.

NEATNESS COUNTS
Surely you've spent hours grooming your dog to perfection for the show ring, but don't forget about yourself! While the dog should be the center of attention, it is important that you also appear neat and clean. Wear smart, appropriate clothes and comfortable shoes in a color that contrasts with your dog's coat. Look and act like a professional.

OBEDIENCE TRIALS
Obedience trials in the US trace back to the early 1930s when organized obedience training was developed to demonstrate how well dog and owner could work together. The pioneer of obedience trials is Mrs. Helen Whitehouse Walker, a Standard Poodle fancier, who designed a series of exercises after the Associated Sheep, Police Army Dog Society of Great Britain. Since the days of Mrs. Walker, obedience trials have grown by leaps and bounds, and today there are over 2,000 trials held in the US every

year, with more than 100,000 dogs competing. Any registered AKC dog can enter an obedience trial, regardless of conformational disqualifications or neutering.

Obedience trials are divided into three levels of progressive difficulty. At the first level, the Novice, dogs compete for the title Companion Dog (CD); at the intermediate level, the Open, dogs compete for the title Companion Dog Excellent (CDX); and at the advanced level, the Utility, dogs compete for the title Utility Dog (UD). Classes are sub-divided into "A" (for beginners) and "B" (for more experienced handlers). A perfect score at any level is 200, and a dog must score 170 or better to earn a "leg," of which three are needed to earn the title. To earn points, the dog must score more than 50% of the available points in each exercise; the possible points range from 20 to 40.

Each level consists of a different set of exercises. In the Novice level, the dog must heel on and off lead, come, long sit, long down and stand for examination.

Your Chessie must be trained to stand still and remain calm while awaiting the judge's inspection.

These skills are the basic ones required for a well-behaved "Companion Dog." The Open level requires that the dog perform the same exercises as in the Novice, but without a leash for extended lengths of time, as well as retrieve a dumbbell, broad jump and drop on recall. In the Utility level, dogs must perform ten difficult exercises, including scent discrimination, hand signals for basic commands, directed jump and directed retrieve.

Once a dog has earned the UD title, he can compete with other proven obedience dogs for the coveted title of Utility Dog Excellent (UDX), which requires that the dog win "legs" in ten shows. Utility Dogs who earn "legs" in Open B and Utility B earn points toward their Obedience Trial Champion title. In 1977, the title Obedience Trial Champion (OTCh.)

WATER TESTS

Most countries offer some type of water test for Chessies and other water breeds, which include the retriever breeds as well as the Portuguese Water Dog, Perro de Agua Español (Spanish Water Dog) and other such aquatic wonders.

Clearing the high jump during a retrieve at an obedience event, this Chessie is a fine example of the breed's trainability and agility.

TEMPERAMENT PLUS

Although it seems that physical conformation is the only factor considered in the show ring, temperament is also of utmost importance. An aggressive or fearful dog should not be shown, as bad behavior will not be tolerated and may pose a threat to the judge, other exhibitors, you and your dog.

was established by the AKC. To become an OTCh., a dog needs to earn 100 points, which requires three first places in Open B and Utility under three different judges.

The Grand Prix of obedience trials, the AKC National Obedience Invitational gives qualifying Utility Dogs the chance to win the newest and highest title: National Obedience Champion (NOC). Only the top 25 ranked obedience dogs, plus any dog ranked in the top 3 in his breed, are allowed to compete.

AGILITY TRIALS

Having had its origins in the UK back in 1977, AKC agility had its official beginning in the US in August 1994, when the first licensed agility trials were held. The AKC allows all registered breeds (including Miscellaneous Class breeds) to participate, providing the dog is 12 months of age or older. Agility is designed so that the handler demonstrates how well the dog can work at his side.

The handler directs his dog over an obstacle course that includes jumps as well as tires, the dog walk, weave poles, pipe tunnels, collapsed tunnels, etc. While working his way through the course, the dog must keep one eye and ear on the handler and the rest of his body on the course. The handler gives verbal and hand signals to guide the dog through the course.

The first organization to promote agility trials in the US was the United States Dog Agility Association, Inc. (USDAA), which was established in 1986 and spawned numerous member clubs around the country. Both the USDAA and the AKC offer titles to winning dogs. Three titles are available through the USDAA: Agility Dog (AD), Advanced Agility Dog (AAD) and Master Agility Dog (MAD). The AKC offers Novice Agility (NA), Open Agility (OA), Agility Excellent (AX) and Master Agility Excellent (MX). Beyond these four AKC titles, dogs can win additional ones in "jumper" classes, Jumpers with Weave Novice (NAJ), Open (OAJ) and Excellent (MXJ), which lead to the ultimate title(s): MACH, Master Agility Champion. Dogs can continue to add number designations to the MACH titles, indicating how many times the dog has met the MACH requirements, such as MACH1, MACH2, etc.

Agility is great fun for dog and owner with many rewards for everyone involved. Interested

A GENTLEMAN'S SPORT

Whether or not your dog wins top honors, showing is a pleasant social event. Sometimes, one may meet a troublemaker or nasty exhibitor, but these people should be ignored and forgotten. In the extremely rare case that someone threatens or harasses you or your dog, you can lodge a complaint with the hosting kennel club. This should be done with extreme prudence. Complaints are investigated seriously and should never be filed on a whim.

owners should join a training club that has obstacles and experienced agility handlers who can introduce you and your dog to the "ropes" (and tires, tunnels, etc.).

TRACKING

Any dog is capable of tracking, using his nose to follow a trail. Tracking tests are exciting and competitive ways to test your Chesapeake's instinctive scenting ability and his ability to search and rescue. The AKC started tracking tests in 1937, when the first AKC-licensed test took place as part of the Utility level at an obedience trial. Ten years later in 1947, the AKC offered the first title, Tracking Dog (TD). It was not until 1980 that the AKC added the title Tracking Dog Excellent (TDX), which was followed by the title Versatile Surface Tracking (VST) in 1995. The title Champion Tracker (CT) is awarded to a dog who has earned all three titles.

In the beginning level of tracking, the owner follows the dog through a field on a long lead. To earn the TD title, the dog must follow a track laid by a human 30 to 120 minutes prior. The track is about 500 yards with up to 5 directional changes. The TDX requires that the dog follow a track that is 3 to 5 hours old over a course up to 1,000 yards with up to 7 directional changes. The VST requires that the dog follow a track up to 5 hours old through an urban setting.

FIELD TRIALS

Field trials are offered to the retrievers, pointers and spaniel breeds of the Sporting Group as well as to the Beagles, Dachshunds and Bassets of the Hound Group. The purpose of field trials is to demonstrate a dog's ability to perform his breed's original purpose in the field. The events vary depending on the type of dog, but in all trials dogs compete against one another for placement and for points toward their Field Champion (FC) titles. Dogs that earn their FC titles plus their championship in the conformation ring are known as Dual Champions; this is extremely prestigious, as it shows that the dog is the ideal blend of form and function, excelling in both areas.

Retriever field trials, designed to simulate "an ordinary day's shoot," are popular and likely the most demanding of these trials. Dogs must "mark" the location of downed feather game and then return the birds to the shooter. Successful dogs are able to "mark" the downed game by remembering where the bird fell as well as correct use of the wind and terrain. Dogs are tested both on land and water.

Difficulty levels are based on the number of birds downed as well as the number of "blind retrieves" (where a bird is placed away from the view of the dog and the handler directs the dog by the use of hand signals and verbal commands). The term "Non-Slip" retriever, often applied to these trials, refers to a dog that is steady at the handler's side until commanded to go. Every field trial includes four stakes of increasing levels of difficulty. Each stake is judged by a team of two judges who look for many natural abilities, including steadiness, courage, style, control and training.

HUNTING TESTS

Hunting tests are not competitive like field trials, and participating dogs are judged against a standard like in a conformation show. The first hunting tests were devised by the North American Hunting Retriever Association (NAHRA) as an alternative to field trials for retriever owners to appreciate their dogs' natural innate ability in the field without the expense and pressure of a formal field trial. The intent of hunting tests is the same as that of field trials, to test the dog's ability in a simulated hunting scenario.

The AKC instituted its hunting tests in June 1985 and popularity has grown. The AKC offers three titles at hunting tests, Junior Hunter (JH), Senior Hunter (SH) and Master Hunter (MH). Each title requires that the dog earn qualifying "legs" at the tests: the JH requiring four; the SH, five; and the MH, six. In addition to the AKC, the United Kennel Club also offers hunting tests through its affiliate club, the Hunting Retriever Club, Inc. (HRC), which began the tests in 1984.

A natural combination of skill and style, the Chessie makes a striking impression in all areas of the dog sport.

CHESAPEAKE BAY RETRIEVER

As a Chesapeake owner, you have selected your dog so that you and your loved ones can have a companion, a protector, a hunter and a four-legged family member. You invest time, money and effort to care for and train the family's new charge. Of course, this chosen canine behaves perfectly! Well, perfectly like a *dog*.

THINK LIKE A DOG
Dogs do not think like humans, nor do humans think like dogs, though we try. Unfortunately, a dog is incapable of comprehending how humans think, so the responsibility falls on the owner to adopt a viable canine mindset. Dogs cannot rationalize and they only exist in the present moment. Many a dog owner makes the mistake in training of thinking that he can reprimand his dog for something the dog did a while ago. Basically, you cannot even reprimand a dog for something he did 20 seconds ago! Either catch him in the act or forget it! It is a waste of your and your dog's time—in his mind, you are reprimanding him for

whatever he is doing at that moment.

The following behavioral problems represent some which owners most commonly encounter. Every dog is unique and every situation is unique. No author could purport for you to solve your Chesapeake's problems simply by reading a script. Here we outline some basic "dogspeak" so that owners' chances of solving behavioral problems are improved.

Discuss bad habits with your veterinarian and he can recommend a behavioral specialist to consult in appropriate cases. Since behavioral abnormalities are the main reason for owners' abandoning their pets, we hope that you will make a valiant effort to solve your Chesapeake's problems. Patience and understanding are virtues that must dwell in every pet-loving household.

AGGRESSION
This is a problem that concerns all responsible dog owners. Aggression can be a problem in

dogs of any breed, even those not known as aggressive, and, when not controlled, always becomes dangerous. An aggressive dog, no matter the size, may lunge at, bite or even attack a person or another dog. Aggressive behavior is not to be tolerated. It is more than just inappropriate behavior; it is painful for a family to watch their dog become unpredictable in his behavior to the point where they are afraid of him. While not all aggressive behavior is dangerous, things like growling, baring teeth, etc., can be frightening. It is important to ascertain why the dog is acting in this manner. Aggression is a display of dominance, and the dog should not have the dominant role in his pack, which is, in this case, your family.

It is important not to challenge an aggressive dog, as this could provoke an attack. Observe your Chesapeake's body language. Does he make direct eye contact and stare? Does he try to make himself as large as possible: ears pricked, chest out, tail erect?

Height and size signify authority in a dog pack—being taller or "above" another dog literally means that he is "above" in social status. These body signals tell you that your Chesapeake thinks he is in charge, a problem that needs to be addressed. An aggressive dog is unpredictable; you never know when he is going to strike and what he is going to do. You cannot understand why a dog that is playful one minute is growling the next.

Fear is a common cause of aggression in dogs. Perhaps your Chesapeake had a negative experience as a puppy, which causes him to be fearful when a similar situation presents itself later in life. The dog may act aggressively in order to protect himself from whatever is making

The challenge of training any dog is to understand how he thinks. Chessies are intelligent, perceptive dogs that need responsive, interactive owners.

TUG-OF-WAR

You should never play tug-of-war games with your puppy. Such games create a struggle for "top dog" position and teach the puppy that it is okay to challenge you. It will also encourage your puppy's natural tendency to bite down hard and *win*.

him afraid. It is not always easy to determine what is making your dog fearful, but if you can isolate what brings out the fear reaction, you can help the dog get over it.

Supervise your Chesapeake's interactions with people and other dogs, and praise the dog when it goes well. If he starts to act aggressively in a situation, correct him and remove him from the situation. Do not let people approach the dog and start petting him without your express permission. That way, you can have the dog sit to accept petting, and praise him when he behaves properly. You are focusing on praise and on modifying his behavior by rewarding him when he acts appropriately. By being gentle and by supervising his interactions, you are showing him that there is no need to be afraid or defensive.

The best solution is to consult a behavioral specialist, one who has experience with the Chesapeake if possible. Together, perhaps you can pinpoint the

cause of your dog's aggression and do something about it. An aggressive dog cannot be trusted, and a dog that cannot be trusted is not safe to have as a family pet. If, very unusually, you find that your pet has become untrustworthy and you feel it necessary to seek a new home with a more suitable family and environment, explain fully to the new owners all your reasons for rehoning the dog to be fair to all concerned.

AGGRESSION TOWARD OTHER DOGS
Some Chessies can be somewhat dog-aggressive, though a well-bred, properly trained and socialized dog should get on well with other dogs. Every dog is different, and caution is always advised when dealing with a dog that may be potentially aggressive. A dog's aggressive behavior toward another dog stems from not enough exposure to other dogs at an early age. If other dogs make your Chesapeake nervous and agitated, he will lash out as a protective mechanism. A dog that has not received sufficient exposure to other canines tends to think that he is the only dog on the planet. The animal becomes so dominant that he does not even show signs that he is fearful or threatened. Without growling or any other physical signal as a warning, he will lunge at and bite the other dog.

A way to correct this is to let

your Chesapeake approach another dog when walking on lead. Watch very closely and, at the first sign of aggression, correct your Chesapeake and pull him away. Scold him for any sign of discomfort, and then praise him when he ignores the other dog. Keep this up until he either stops the aggressive behavior, learns to ignore other dogs or accepts other dogs. Praise him lavishly for his correct behavior.

DOMINANT AGGRESSION

A social hierarchy is firmly established in a wild dog pack. The dog wants to dominate those under him and please those above him. Dogs know that there must be a leader. If you are not the obvious choice for emperor, the dog will assume the throne! These conflicting innate desires are what a dog owner is up against when he sets about training a dog. In training a dog to obey commands, the owner is reinforcing that he is the top dog in the "pack" and that the dog

Know your Chessie's body language. Since Chessies rarely have a problem with aggressive behavior, it would be unusual for you to see your dog posing a threat to you, strangers or other dogs, unless challenged.

should, and should want to, serve his superior. Thus, the owner is suppressing the dog's urge to dominate by modifying his behavior and making him obedient.

With a dominant dog, punishment and negative reinforcement can have the opposite effect of what you are after. It can make a dog fearful and/or act out aggressively if he feels he is being challenged. Remember, a dominant dog perceives himself at the top of the social heap, and will fight to defend his perceived status. The best way to prevent that is to never give him reason to think that he is in control in the first place.

If you are having trouble

DOMINANT BEHAVIOR

Never allow your puppy to growl at you or bare his tiny teeth. Such behavior is dominant and aggressive. If not corrected, the dog will repeat the behavior, which will become more threatening as he grows larger and will eventually lead to biting.

training your Chesapeake and it seems as if he is constantly challenging your authority, seek the help of an obedience trainer or behavioral specialist. A professional will work with both you and your dog to teach you effective techniques to use at home. Beware of trainers who rely on excessively harsh methods; scolding is necessary now and then, but the focus in your training should always be on positive reinforcement.

SEXUAL BEHAVIOR

Dogs exhibit certain sexual behaviors that may have influenced your choice of male or female when you first purchased your Chesapeake. To a certain extent, spaying/neutering will eliminate these behaviors, but if you are purchasing a dog that you wish to breed from, you should be aware of what you will have to deal with throughout your Chessie's life.

Female dogs usually have two estruses per year, with each season lasting about three weeks. These are the only times in which a female dog will mate, and she usually will not allow this until the second week of the cycle, although this varies from bitch to bitch. If not bred during the heat cycle, it is not uncommon for a bitch to experience a false pregnancy, in which her mammary glands swell and

IT'S PLAY TIME
Physical games like pulling contests, wrestling, jumping and teasing should not be encouraged. Inciting a dog's crazy behavior tends to confuse him. The owner has to be able to control his dog at all times. Even in play, your dog has to know that you are the leader and that you decide when to play and when to behave mannerly.

she exhibits maternal tendencies toward toys or other objects.

With male dogs, owners must be aware that whole dogs (dogs who are not neutered) have the natural inclination to mark their territory. Males mark their territory by spraying small amounts of urine as they lift their legs in a macho ritual. Marking can occur both outdoors in the yard and around the neighborhood as well as indoors on furniture legs, curtains and the sofa. Such behavior can be very frustrating for the owner; early training is strongly urged before the "urge" strikes your dog. Neutering the male at an appropriate early age can solve this problem before it becomes a habit.

Other problems associated with males are wandering and mounting. Both of these habits, of course, belong to the unneutered dog, whose sexual drive leads him away from home in search of the bitch in heat. Males will mount females in heat, as well as any other dog, male or female, that happens to catch their fancy. Other possible mounting partners include his owner, the furniture, guests to the home and friends on the street. Discourage such behavior early on.

Owners must further recognize that mounting is not merely a sexual expression but also one of dominance, which can be exhibited in males and females alike. Be consistent and be persistent, and you will find that you can "move mounters."

CHEWING

The national canine pastime is chewing! Every dog loves to sink his "canines" into a tasty bone, but if a bone's not available, just about anything will do! Dogs need to chew, to massage their gums, to make their new teeth feel better and to exercise their jaws. This is a natural behavior that is deeply embedded in all things canine. Your role as owner is not to stop the dog's chewing, but rather to redirect it to positive, chew-worthy objects. Be an informed owner and purchase proper chew toys, like strong nylon bones that will not splinter. Be sure that the objects are safe and durable, since your dog's safety is at risk. Again, the owner is responsible for ensuring a dog-proof environment.

The best answer is prevention; that is, put your shoes, handbags and other tasty objects in their proper places (out of the reach of the growing canine mouth). Direct your puppy to his toys whenever you see him "tasting" the furniture legs or the leg of your trousers. Make a loud noise to attract the pup's attention and immediately escort him to his chew toy and engage him with the toy for at least four minutes, praising and encouraging him all the while. An array of safe, interesting chew toys will keep your dog's mind and teeth occupied, and distracted from chewing on things he shouldn't.

BITTER BITERS
Some trainers recommend deterrents, such as hot pepper, a bitter spice or a product designed for this purpose, to discourage the dog from chewing unwanted objects. Test these products to see which works best before investing in large quantities.

JUMPING UP

Jumping up is a dog's friendly way of saying hello! Some dog owners do not mind when their dog jumps up. The problem arises when guests come to the house and the dog greets them in the same manner—whether they like it or not! However friendly the greeting may be, the chances are that your visitors will not appreciate such enthusiasm from a dog as large as the Chessie. The dog will not be able to distinguish upon whom he can jump and whom he cannot. Therefore, it is probably best to discourage this behavior entirely.

Pick a command such as "Off" (avoid using "Down" since you will use that for the dog to lie down) and tell him "Off" when he jumps up. Place him on the ground on all fours and have him sit, praising him the whole time. Always lavish him with praise and petting when he is in the sit position. In this way, you can give him an affectionate greeting, let him know that you are as pleased to see him as he is to see you and instill good manners at the same time!

DIGGING

Digging, which is seen as a destructive behavior to humans, is actually quite a natural behavior in dogs. Although the terriers (the "earth dogs") are most associated with digging, any dog's desire to dig can be irrepressible and most frustrating to his owners.

When digging occurs in your yard, it is actually a normal behavior redirected into something the dog can do in his everyday life. In the wild, a dog would be actively seeking food, making his own shelter, etc. He would be using his paws in a purposeful manner for his survival. Since you provide him with food and shelter, he has no need to use his paws for these purposes, and so the energy that he would be using may manifest itself in the form of little holes all over your yard and flower beds.

Perhaps your dog is digging as a reaction to boredom—it is somewhat similar to someone eating a whole bag of chips in front of the TV—because they are there and there is nothing better to do! Basically, the answer is to provide the dog with adequate

I'M HOME!

Dogs left alone for varying lengths of time may often react wildly when their owners return. Sometimes they run, jump, bite, chew, tear things apart, wet themselves, gobble their food or behave in very undisciplined ways. If your dog behaves in this manner upon your return home, allow him to calm down before greeting him or he will consider your attention as a reward for his antics.

play and exercise so that his mind and paws are occupied, and so that he feels as if he is doing something useful.

Of course, digging is easiest to control if it is stopped as soon as possible, but it is often hard to catch a dog in the act. If your dog is a compulsive digger and is not easily distracted by other activities, you can designate an area on your property where he is allowed to dig. If you catch him digging in an off-limits area of the yard, immediately bring him to the approved area and praise him for digging there. Keep a close eye on him so that you can catch him in the act—that is the only way to make him understand what is permitted and what is not. If you take him to a hole he dug an hour ago and tell him "No," he will understand that you are not fond of holes, dirt or flowers. If you catch him while he is stifle-deep in your tulips, that is when he will get your message.

SEPARATION ANXIETY

Recognized by behaviorists as the most common form of stress for dogs, separation anxiety can also lead to destructive behaviors in your dog. It's more than your Chessie's howling his displeasure at your leaving the house and his being left alone. This is a normal reaction, no different from the child who cries as his mother

A Chessie given productive exercise to keep him busy should not develop destructive or otherwise inappropriate behavior.

leaves him on the first day at school. Separation anxiety is more serious. In fact, if you are constantly with your dog, he will come to expect you with him all of the time, making it even more traumatic for him when you are not there.

Obviously, you enjoy spending time with your dog, and he thrives on your love and attention. However, it should not become a dependent relationship in which he is heartbroken without you. This broken heart can also bring on destructive behavior as well as loss of appetite, depression and lack of interest in play and interaction.

PHARMACEUTICAL FIX

There are two drugs specifically designed to treat mental problems in dogs. About seven million dogs each year are destroyed because owners can no longer tolerate their dogs' behavior, according to Nicholas Dodman, a specialist in animal behavior at Tufts University in Massachusetts.

The first drug, Clomicalm, is prescribed for dogs suffering from separation anxiety, which is said to cause them to react when left alone by barking, chewing their owners' belongings, drooling copiously or defecating or urinating inside the home.

The second drug, Anipryl, is recommended for cognitive dysfunction syndrome or "old dog syndrome," a mental deterioration that comes with age. Such dogs often seem to forget that they were housebroken and where their food bowls are, and they may even fail to recognize their owners.

A tremendous human-animal bonding relationship is established with all dogs, particularly senior dogs. This precious relationship deteriorates when the dog does not recognize his master. The drug can restore the bond and make senior dogs feel more like their "old selves."

Canine behaviorists have been spending much time and energy to help owners better understand the significance of this stressful condition.

One thing you can do to minimize separation anxiety is to make your entrances and exits as low-key as possible. Do not give your dog a long drawn-out goodbye, and do not lavish him with hugs and kisses when you return. This is giving in to the attention that he craves, and it will only make him miss it more when you are away. Another thing you can try is to give your dog a treat when you leave; this will not only keep him occupied and keep his mind off the fact that you have just left, but it will also help him associate your leaving with a pleasant, positive experience.

You may have to accustom your dog to being left alone in intervals. Of course, when your dog starts whimpering as you approach the door, your first instinct will be to run to him and comfort him, but do not do it! Eventually he will adjust to your absence. His anxiety stems from being placed in an unfamiliar situation; by familiarizing him with being alone, he will learn that he will survive. That is not to say you should purposely leave your dog home alone, but the dog needs to know that, while he can depend on you for his care, you do not have to be by his side 24 hours a day. Some behaviorists recommend tiring the dog out before you leave home—take him for a walk or engage in a game of fetch in the yard.

When the dog is alone in the house, he should be placed in his crate—another distinct advantage to crate training your dog. The crate should be placed in his familiar happy family area, where he normally sleeps and already feels comfortable, thereby making him feel more at ease when he is alone. Be sure to give the dog a special chew toy to enjoy while he settles into his crate.

BARKING

Dogs cannot talk—oh, what they would say if they could! Instead, barking is a dog's way of "talking." It can be somewhat frustrating because it is not always easy to tell what a dog means by his bark—is he excited, happy, frightened or angry? Whatever it is that the dog is trying to say, he should not be punished for barking. It is only when the barking becomes excessive, and when the excessive barking becomes a bad habit, that the behavior needs to be modified.

Fortunately, Chesapeakes are not vocal dogs; they will bark at strangers if encouraged to do so. This type of barking is purposeful and should never be discouraged. If an intruder came into your home in the middle of the night and your Chesapeake barked a

warning, wouldn't you be pleased? You would probably deem your dog a hero, a wonderful guardian and protector of the home. On the other hand, if a friend drops by unexpectedly, rings the doorbell and is greeted with a sudden sharp bark, you would probably be annoyed at the dog. But in reality, isn't this just the same behavior? The dog does not know any better. Unless he sees who is at the door and it is someone he knows, he will bark as a means of vocalizing that his (and your) territory is being threatened. While your friend is not posing a threat, it is all the same to the dog. Barking is his means of letting you know that there is an intrusion, whether friend or foe, on your property. This type of barking is instinctive and should not be discouraged.

Excessive habitual barking, however, is a problem that should be corrected early on. As your Chesapeake grows up, you will be able to tell when his barking is purposeful and when it is for no reason. You will become able to distinguish your dog's different barks and their meanings. For example, the bark when someone comes to the door will be different from the bark when he is excited to see you. It is similar to a person's tone of voice, except that the dog has to rely totally on tone of voice because he does not have the benefit of using words.

QUIET ON THE SET

To encourage proper barking, you can teach your dog the command "Quiet." When someone comes to the door and the dog barks a few times, praise him. Talk to him soothingly and, when he stops barking, tell him "Quiet" and continue to praise him. In this sense, you are letting him bark his warning, which is an instinctive behavior, and then rewarding him for being quiet after a few barks. You may initially reward him with a treat after he has been quiet for a few minutes.

An incessant barker will be evident at an early age.

There are some things that encourage a dog to bark. For example, if your dog barks non-stop for a few minutes and you give him a treat to quiet him, he believes that you are rewarding him for barking. He will associate barking with getting a treat and will keep doing it until he is rewarded. On the other hand, if you give him a command such as "Quiet" and praise him after he has stopped barking for a few seconds, he will get the idea that being "quiet" is what you want him to do.

FOOD STEALING

Is your dog devising ways of stealing food from your coffee table or kitchen counter? If so, you must answer the following questions: Is your Chesapeake hungry, or is he "constantly famished" like many dogs seem to be? Face it, some dogs are more food-motivated than others. They are totally obsessed by the smell of food and can only think of their next meal. Food stealing is terrific fun and always yields a great reward—*food*, glorious food.

Your goal as an owner, therefore, is to be sensible about where food is placed in the home and to reprimand your dog whenever he is caught in the act of stealing. But remember, only reprimand your dog if you actually see him stealing, not later when the crime is discovered; that will be of no use at all and will only serve to confuse him.

BEGGING

Just like food stealing, begging is a favorite pastime of hungry puppies! It achieves that same lovely result—*food!* Dogs quickly learn that their owners keep the "good food" for themselves, and that we humans do not dine on dry food alone. Begging is a conditioned response related to a specific stimulus, time and place. The sounds of the kitchen, cans and bottles opening, crinkling bags, the smell of food in preparation, etc., will excite the dog, and soon the paws will be in the air!

Here is the solution to stopping this behavior: Never give in to a beggar! You are rewarding the dog for sitting pretty, jumping up, whining and rubbing his nose into you by giving him food. By ignoring the dog, you will (eventually) force the behavior into extinction. Note that the behavior is likely to get worse before it disappears, so be sure there are not any "softies" in the family who will give in to little "Oliver" every time he whimpers, "More, please."

COPROPHAGIA

Feces eating is, to humans, one of the most disgusting behaviors that their dogs could engage in, yet, to dogs, it is perfectly normal. It is hard for us to understand why a dog would want to eat his own feces. He could be seeking certain nutrients that are missing from his diet, he could be just plain hungry or he could be attracted by the pleasing (to a dog) scent. While coprophagia most often refers to the dog's eating his own feces, a dog may just as likely eat that of another animal if he comes across it. Dogs often find the stool of cats and horses more palatable than that of other dogs.

Vets have found that diets with low levels of digestibility, containing relatively low levels of fiber and high levels of starch, increase coprophagia. Therefore, high-fiber diets may decrease the likelihood of dogs' eating feces. Both the consistency of the stool (how firm it feels in the dog's mouth) and the presence of undigested nutrients increase the likelihood. Once the dog develops diarrhea from feces eating, he will likely stop this distasteful habit.

To discourage this behavior, first make sure that the food you are feeding your dog is nutritionally complete and that he is getting enough food. If changes in his diet do not seem to work, and no medical cause can be found, you will have to modify the behavior through environmental control before it becomes a habit. The best way to prevent your dog from eating his stool is to make it unavailable—clean up after he eliminates and remove any stool from the yard. If it is not there, he cannot eat it.

Reprimanding for stool eating rarely impresses the dog. Vets recommend distracting the dog while he is in the act of stool eating. Coprophagia is seen most frequently in pups 6 to 12 months of age, and usually disappears around the dog's first birthday.

INDEX

Page numbers in **boldface** indicate illustrations.

My Chesapeake Bay Retriever

PUT YOUR PUPPY'S FIRST PICTURE HERE

Dog's Name _____

Date _____ Photographer _____